Cambridge Elements

Elements in Ancient Egypt in Context
edited by
Gianluca Miniaci
University of Pisa
Juan Carlos Moreno García
CNRS, Paris
Anna Stevens
University of Cambridge and Monash University

MONARCHIES AND THE ORGANIZATION OF POWER

Ancient Egypt and Babylonia Compared (2100–1750 BC)

Juan Carlos Moreno García
CNRS, Paris

Seth Richardson
The University of Chicago

Shaftesbury Road, Cambridge CB2 8EA, United Kingdom

One Liberty Plaza, 20th Floor, New York, NY 10006, USA

477 Williamstown Road, Port Melbourne, VIC 3207, Australia

314–321, 3rd Floor, Plot 3, Splendor Forum, Jasola District Centre, New Delhi – 110025, India

103 Penang Road, #05–06/07, Visioncrest Commercial, Singapore 238467

Cambridge University Press is part of Cambridge University Press & Assessment, a department of the University of Cambridge.

We share the University's mission to contribute to society through the pursuit of education, learning and research at the highest international levels of excellence.

www.cambridge.org
Information on this title: www.cambridge.org/9781009598200
DOI: 10.1017/9781009025591

© Juan Carlos Moreno García and Seth Richardson 2025

This publication is in copyright. Subject to statutory exception and to the provisions of relevant collective licensing agreements, no reproduction of any part may take place without the written permission of Cambridge University Press & Assessment.

When citing this work, please include a reference to the DOI 10.1017/9781009025591

First published 2025

A catalogue record for this publication is available from the British Library

ISBN 978-1-009-59820-0 Hardback
ISBN 978-1-009-01201-0 Paperback
ISSN 2516-4813 (online)
ISSN 2516-4805 (print)

Cambridge University Press & Assessment has no responsibility for the persistence or accuracy of URLs for external or third-party internet websites referred to in this publication and does not guarantee that any content on such websites is, or will remain, accurate or appropriate.

For EU product safety concerns, contact us at Calle de José Abascal, 56, 1°, 28003 Madrid, Spain, or email eugpsr@cambridge.org

Monarchies and the Organization of Power

Ancient Egypt and Babylonia Compared (2100–1750 BC)

Elements in Ancient Egypt in Context

DOI: 10.1017/9781009025591
First published online: April 2025

Juan Carlos Moreno García
CNRS, Paris

Seth Richardson
The University of Chicago

Author for correspondence: Juan Carlos Moreno García,
jcmorenogarciaaguirre@gmail.com

Abstract: This Element explores the organization of power in ancient Egypt and Mesopotamia and the interaction of diverse social actors between 2100 and 1750 BC. On the one hand, the forms of integration of towns and villages in larger political entities and the role played by local authorities, with a focus on local agency, the influence of mobile populations, the exercise of power in small localities, and the contrast between power reality and royal ideological claims, be they legal, divinely sanctioned, or other. On the other hand, the modalities of penetration of the royal authority in the local sphere, the alliances that linked court dignitaries and local potentates, and the co-option of local leaders. Finally, the influence of such networks of power on the historical evolution of the monarchies and the adaptability of the latter in coping with the challenges they faced to assert and reproduce their authority.

Keywords: Egypt, Babylonia, Middle Bronze Age, ancient states, comparative history

© Juan Carlos Moreno García and Seth Richardson 2025

ISBNs: 9781009598200 (HB), 9781009012010 (PB), 9781009025591 (OC)
ISSNs: 2516-4813 (online), 2516-4805 (print)

Contents

1 Introduction   1

2 The Organization of Power in Babylonia: Problems and Prospects   2

3 Power Organization in Egypt   40

4 Conclusions   75

   References   79

1 Introduction

The end of the third millennium BC was a time of considerable changes in Egypt and the Near East. The previous centuries had seen the consolidation of large polities based on a complex bureaucratic structure both in the Nile Valley and Mesopotamia. In the case of Egypt, the administrative organization of the kingdom expanded and diversified after the construction of the great pyramids at Giza (roughly after 2500 BC): more governmental departments, more officials and scribes, tighter control of the provinces and their resources, and a plethora of rank and function titles. As for the Near East, large supra-regional polities unified Mesopotamia and, occasionally, adjacent areas as well. The old city-state system was replaced by new political forms, more encompassing and, apparently, more intensive in their exercise of power over an incomparable more extended territory. Perhaps not by chance, these transformations coincided with the expansion of trading and exchange networks over vast areas in the second half of the third millennium BC, with Egyptians involved in the Levant and north-eastern Africa (Nubia, Punt and beyond). At the same time, Mesopotamian activities extended toward Anatolia, the Middle East, Arabia, and India. Both spheres were connected through major trading cities like Byblos and Ebla.

Then, these early "imperial" formations experienced a transformation into lesser-scale polities, a process that overlapped only partially in both regions. When the Egyptian monarchy disintegrated around 2160 BC, more or less at the same time as the Akkadian Empire, this was hardly the traumatic process imagined by earlier scholars. Some regions of Egypt thrived, particularly in the north, now organized as the regional Heracleopolitan kingdom, encompassing part of the Delta, the Fayum and most of Middle Egypt. In the case of Mesopotamia, the process was more gradual. The relatively short-lived Ur III monarchy still managed to control part of the former Akkadian Empire, but it disintegrated by 2004 BC and was replaced by several competing kingdoms. Meanwhile, Egypt was reunified again around 2050 BC or slightly afterward. However, the newly restored monarchy faced considerable opposition in some regions, had to cope with regional lords who held their own political and economic agendas and failed to create a tax system capable of capturing resources at the same scale as in the third millennium BC. After two centuries of unification, the country entered again into a long period of political fragmentation shortly after 1800 BC.

Whereas both regions remained distinctive and direct contact between them – diplomatic or economic – was marginal, they experienced similar vicissitudes despite differences in their political organization and socio-economic relations.

This opens a fascinating window for comparative research that may help place both regions and their respective societies in a broader perspective and help us to understand early political dynamics: How did these state societies react to the increase and extension of exchange networks? Did specific urban sectors influence decision-making, even limit royal agency? Was centralization more apparent than real, such that other social forces had the potential of shaping power and limiting royal agency? What was the role of mobile and "marginal" people in these transformations? Which mechanisms favored the accumulation and circulation of wealth, and to what extent did kings succeed in capturing, even monopolizing, critical resources and depriving potential rivals of doing the same? Did the palatial sphere impose its cultural values and normative codes easily outside the narrow circle of the court, or, on the contrary, were they challenged by alternative practices deeply rooted in society?

Thus, by comparing ancient Mesopotamia (Seth Richardson) and Egypt (Juan Carlos Moreno García) during a specific period – the late third and early second millennia BC – we analyze the possibilities, challenges, and limits in the construction of power experienced by two Near Eastern societies (see also the inspiring work by Baines and Yoffee 1998). Behind a façade of robust kingship and centralized authority, it may be possible to grasp other realities in which power, wealth and status were negotiated and distributed between different actors and through various channels. From this perspective, what appears, superficially, to be highly idiosyncratic societies may reveal unexpectedly shared features and structural differences that can open helpful venues for comparative analysis of statehood in the ancient Near East. In the following sections, "comparison" means exactly that: an assessment of disparities as well as similarities. We do not find that the cultures under study were either essentially the same or too different to compare. What these societies may have had most in common were challenges of similar kinds: finding balances of state, civic, and private power, overcoming barriers of distance, and using both material wealth and ideological persuasion to produce a coherent and organized sense of governance.

2 The Organization of Power in Babylonia: Problems and Prospects

The "organization of power" is no new topic for comparative scholarship on ancient Mesopotamia (Figure 1).[1] The conflicts and cooperations between

---

[1] Abbreviations follow *The Assyrian Dictionary of the Oriental Institute of the University of Chicago* (Chicago: The Oriental Institute, 1956–2010). Periods referred to here include the Early Dynastic (2900–2350 BC), Akkadian (2350–2192 BC), Ur III (2112–2004 BC), Old Babylonian (2004–1595 BC), Kassite (ca. 1475–1155 BC), and Neo-Babylonian (626–539 BC).

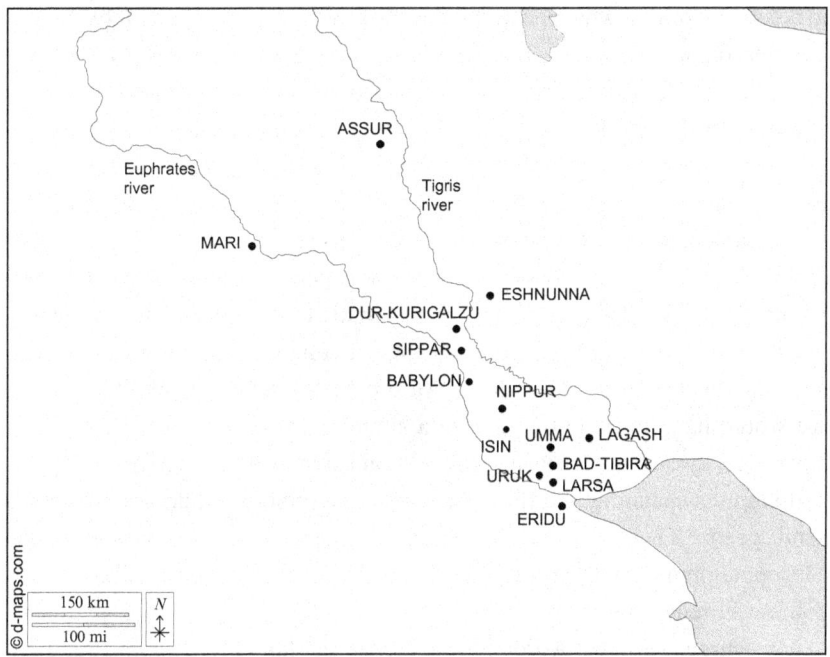

Figure 1 Map of Mesopotamia (©Juan Carlos Moreno García).

different nodes and levels of political authority that lay at the center of early state-building projects have long attracted the attention of historians working in both history and archaeology. Mesopotamia, as one of the earliest known state societies, obviously plays an important role in such studies. Attempts to define how power "worked" in early Mesopotamian society have emerged from two general directions: First, from studies of archaeology and economic-administrative texts – essentially social-science approaches, focusing on material goods in the formation of cities, institutions, and agricultural production – and second, from literary approaches, humanities approaches forefronting themes such as kingship, temple religion, and social orders.[2] From these two lines of attack, we have derived two rather divergent pictures of Mesopotamian political culture: one which was almost obsessively committed to administration as a language of control; and another which was preoccupied with lofty theological and ideological notions of kingship and cosmos.

Whether this culture ran from earth to heaven, or heaven to earth, it was an emphatically urban and political one. But it was one of profoundly heterodox

---

[2] E.g., Adams and Kraeling eds. 1960. The Rencontre Assyriologique Internationale has only once focused on "power" (Wilhelm ed. 2012). See also Gibson and Biggs eds.1991, Selz 2007, Bang and Scheidel eds. 2013.

makeup; a world in which power did not have any single defining look, feel, or obvious linguistic, religious, or ethnic self-conception. Across thousands of years of political culture in the Babylonian south – to say nothing here of the Assyrian north, which was a substantially separate cultural formation – Mesopotamian state authority was shaped by such a variety of conditions as to defy general characterization. This political variegation is reflected in the iconographic, linguistic, and even literary-generic diversity of Mesopotamian culture, forms which rarely seemed to jell or sit still long enough to achieve the iconic "look" of power seemingly characteristic (if deceptively so) of Egypt.

This lays down multiple challenges for anyone wanting to make synthetic and general statements. To address "Mesopotamia" as a socio-political whole, we would have to lump together in a single cultural framework the experiences of city-states, territorial states, larger conquest and "national" states, and empires spanning multiple ethnolinguistic regions, all across three thousand years. Thus to speak of a singular or distinctive way in which Mesopotamian power was organized across the *longue durée* will always be somewhat reductive.

My approach will be twofold. First, the reader should be prepared that I will make relatively brief general statements about early state organization as points of departure for more detailed descriptions of the many deviations from those norms. It is important to forefront diversity and heteropraxy *as the norms* of Mesopotamian power, because the exceptions are simply too numerous to be exceptions. Second, I will use the Old Babylonian period (hereafter, "OB") as a template for Mesopotamian state society, though noting differences with other periods along the way. There are good reasons to choose the OB. For one thing, it is the period I know the best; for another, it is roughly contemporary to the time discussed here by Moreno García for Egypt. More substantially, it is the period by which states had had more than a millennium to coalesce their portfolio of claimed powers into forms coherent and well-documented enough to work as an object of analysis. These claims still fell demonstrably short of reality, but they illustrate the early state's fundamentally "presumptive" nature. This is not just to say that states didn't have all the powers they claimed – this observation by itself would be banal – but that the *desire* for those claims to be(come) true was the discursive motor generative of their eventual realization.

I begin with a general and somewhat idealized description of the ways in which power was organized in the OB period – about how it worked ("Paradigms and Models"). I will then turn to some theoretical problems with those archetypes, not only because they impose some limits on our knowledge (as they do), but also because they present opportunities to reinterpret what those limits on knowledge themselves can tell us ("Problems into Possibilities"). In the following sections,

I will consider organized power in different sectors: the central role that cities played in state formation; the attempts of states to territorialize or provincialize the land over which they held sway; the durable presence of nonurban and non-state bases of political power; and the networks of merchants, wealthy households, and temple estates which interacted with but remained autonomous of state power. I am on the watch for structural elements which both furthered and limited the powers of central states. My discussion of the "organization of power" necessarily engages a review of more sectors of society than just royal/state power, but I do limit my interest to the political role of other actors, not to their economic or social power. The word "organization" is therefore as important as "power": Where I discuss merchants, scribes, priests, and judges, it is to assess the roles they played in constructing and exercising *political* power embodied within the state system.

2.1 Paradigms and Models

I am dubious about descriptions of how states work; my view is that they often don't, at least not fully or according to plan. But the ways they *don't* work have the potential to be as informative about political cultures as the ways that they do.

Whatever the approach, I begin with a sense of the main lines along which power was organized in the OB period. Following the demise of the centralized Ur III state, Babylonia was divided between small territorial kingdoms centered on five major cities: Isin, Larsa, Uruk, Babylon, and Ešnunna. (Mari, to the northwest on the Euphrates, was another important peer state, but at a substantial geopolitical distance.) The fortunes of these cities waxed and waned within the period, but none was regionally dominant for more than a generation or two. Alongside these states, dozens of petty kingships sprang up in smaller cities; in some cases, we do not even know where those cities were, or when exactly their kings ruled. The OB is commonly described as one of incessant warfare, but this characterization should be tempered somewhat: Violent interstate competition in lower Mesopotamia was concentrated in the 180 years from 1915–1735 BC, less than half of the 400-year period. Still, the quest to militarily reassert a single hegemon over the lower alluvium following the fall of Ur was the single most important effort to "organize" power, and warfare and conquest remained important to the state project.

Within their local orbit, these Babylonian kingdoms relied on methods of governance used in many other periods. Dynastic palace organizations used subjugation by force to effect rule, but also power-sharing with the cities, temples, and local elites they recruited as clients. Many cities and temples had preexisting traditions and identities, and came equipped with their own lands, clients, and representative bodies (priests, judges, assemblies, etc.). These substructures of power could be co-opted or colonized by ruling dynasties, but they could not be wholly erased or subsumed. Studies of OB Sippar (Harris 1975), Nippur (Stone 1987), and Ur (Van De Mieroop 1992) provide important accounts of these dynamic urban environments and the interlocking communities inhabiting them. As Andrea Seri showed in her 2005 survey of local power, the everyday contact people had with officialdom was with mayors, canal-inspectors, city gatekeepers, and elders, not the viziers, generals, and governors whom those men served (Figure 2). It is thus important to begin with the sense that kings and palaces headed up umbrella organizations under which other

Figure 2 Early Dynastic limestone statue of Ur-Ešlila, a city elder (ab-ba uru) of Adab, dedicated to the god Ninšubur in honor of a local king of Adab named Bara-ḫenidu, ca. 25th/24th BC. Statues like these marked the allegiance of city officials who managed everyday affairs to rulers who were more remote from the populace. ISAC Museum A7447, courtesy of the Institute for the Study of Ancient Cultures of the University of Chicago.

subsidiary bureaus maintained their own discrete local authority. It would be too much to call this a "federal" structure of kingship, but it is important to recognize from the first that distributed sovereignty was the rule.

Outside and beyond the "organelles" of local institutions, Babylonian states built wealth, subjects, and power in much the same way other Mesopotamian states had, both before and afterward: through their control of land (Renger 1995). State land (presumably appropriated) was doled out to clients in exchange for service and in-kind taxes. This practice bound many people at every level of society to the palaces, from individual sharecroppers, to soldiers and workers ready for war and work, to grandees and governors ruling whole districts. Even cities and temples with their own lands were sometimes required to tithe up to the Crown based on the political fiction that their lands were held at the pleasure of the king. Land was thus the foundation of state wealth, far and away its most important asset and source of revenue. Yet palace lands never included *all* the land of any kingdom. We are aware of many private landholders, as well as transhumant and tribally organized groups living outside of or loosely affiliated with state control, and there clearly were significant sedentary rural populations not living under the rule of states at all. To these points, I will return in in what follows.

Particularly interesting is the use by OB states of officers and private factors to convert in-kind taxes – from the agricultural sector (i.e., crops and animals), through loans and sales – into storable institutional wealth in the form of silver. Credit sales and productive loans appear in contracts between private actors, but often the profits went to the palaces as a system of state finance. We do have evidence for similar mechanisms from other periods, but the OB case looks uniquely "privatized." Certainly, the fiscal problem itself was not unique: Mesopotamian states of all periods – indeed every pre-modern state with an agricultural economy – faced the same challenge: There was only so much barley, cheese, meat, and beer any palace could ever store; conversion into non-spoilable wealth was the goal.

Babylonian palaces also built revenue and economic power through secondary production, operating breweries, workshops producing textiles and crafts, harvesting wool and sheepskins, baking bricks, and leasing out draft animals; they operated productive "bureaus" wherever resources and opportunities arose. Many such areas of production were leased out to concessionaires, some of them endowed with titles reflecting rights to produce and collect. States also collected taxes on trade goods, often through "Overseers of the Merchants" stationed in city "harbor" districts (*kārum*s). Imposts were collected on products brought from afar (sometimes paid in gold, the possession of which may have been a state prerogative) just as readily as on local products sold in bulk. The effectiveness of states to capitalize on commercial activities, however, was limited.

The OB has been characterized as an epoch of decentralized power, where state business was largely outsourced to local units, entrepreneurs, agents, and traders. These states were administratively *laissez-faire*, through what has been called the *Palastgeschäft* ("palace business") model (Yoffee 1977). Against this image of detached state control, socioeconomic life outside the state sector seems to have been more robust in this time than it ever had been (and would not be again until the Neo-Babylonian period). Long-distance private trade is documented between Ur and the Persian Gulf (thus connecting Mesopotamia, secondarily, to the Indus River Valley and even central Asia); between Sippar and northern Syria; between Babylonia and the Assyrian trade system running up into Anatolia. The reach, volume, and sheer value of the trade goods (silver, tin, copper, textiles, wine, etc.) are arresting, especially considering that the trading agents in these systems operated privately, mostly outside of state purview.

Closer to home, everyday archival texts paint a picture of a relatively well-to-do private citizenry. Householders in many cities bought and sold land (Figure 3), extended credit, owned slaves and cattle, and passed their estates on to their children through inheritance and into other families through marriage. These practices are reflected in the textual genres that arose to support their increasing autonomy, especially contracts and letters. We see law and epistolary expression reaching much higher degrees of sophistication than in previous ages, and something like an emerging *burgher*-class sensibility. This was also the age in which we find some of the best evidence for political life and power at the local level. City assemblies, town judges, and local notables acting as witnesses show us a citizenry participating in community decision-making. Literary production, too, was in a golden age of sorts, with some of the best-known works in Sumerian copied extensively even as new epics, stories, and scientific literature were being composed in Akkadian. Altogether, we see a powerful palace sector, a vigorous commercial world, an emerging civil society, and a landscape full of non-state tribes and villages. Altogether, this cast of characters must call into question any presumption that states were exclusively in control of "organizing power."

2.2 Problems into Possibilities

One difficulty in analyzing any Mesopotamian state has to do with our own terminology: How easily we assume, from the words in Sumerian and Akkadian for "king" (lugal/*šarru*) and "kingship" (nam-lugal/*šarrūtu*), that an extrapolated

Figure 3 Plan and measurements of three adjacent private houses belonging to men named Kilari, Ḫululḫulul, and Šara-zida. From the Ur III city of Umma (ca. 2050 BC). Alongside the "great households" of palaces and temples, private households became increasingly important nodes of power from the Middle Bronze Age onward. VAT 07026 (Vorderasiatisches Museum, Berlin). Image courtesy of the Cuneiform Digital Library Initiative.

term for "king*doms*"[3] – that is, states – must also have existed. But (importantly) neither language extended the semantic sense to a substantive categorical noun "kingdom," or developed a workable term on any other semantic basis to mean "state," "nation," "country," and so on.[4] I am not making a claim that because the

---

[3] The etymological isometry of king-kingship-kingdom pertains as well in German, French, and Italian, underscoring our expectations that sovereignty is inherently territorialized.

[4] Cf. Akk. *mātu*, "land," as early as the Late Bronze Age, but often in a poetic sense, "when the gods established the land," a "far-off land," etc.

word "kingdom" was absent from the lexicon that the idea did not exist; territorialized states were an important *aspiration* of Mesopotamian polities even if as yet unrealized. But a Mesopotamian state was something substantially organized around a person and an office, not a territory. Babylonian kingship was a political formation in which no political or legal-juristic identity was ever made between royal power, territory, and the things and people "contained" within it. This was largely true for most states even up through the early modern period. To the extent that we (sometimes necessarily) speak about ancient states in these ways is largely a framework imported from assumptions about what countries are and do by the standards of post-1789 AD nation-states. So any talk about "parts" and "wholes" working together for Babylonian antiquities must begin by shedding the erroneous premise that "states" existed as territorialized "wholes": bounded territories within which there were regularized relations of law, political membership, and common markets.

The theoretical work to be done, then, is to try to understand what kingship states which were not "kingdoms" might *be*. Mesopotamian states were palatial estates, great households with assets in the form of clients and properties scattered irregularly throughout the land. These households were preeminent in scale but not in kind, asymmetrically rather than categorically more powerful than the other institutions to which we might compare them (i.e., temples and cities), merely stronger in some functions than in others. The challenge is to examine the interplay of parts without presupposing the totalities we expect of modern nation-states.

Despite the fact that states varied over time, many institutional issues reappeared across periods. The division and distribution of resources and authorities perennially created alliances and tensions between different groups of actors. Mesopotamian politics included relations between palaces, temples, and private households; the king and his court; officials and scribes (noting some overlap); ruling and subject cities; markets and institutions; locals and colonists; herders and farmers; and administrators and dependents. The successful establishment, distribution, and exercise of power required to manage all these groups, resources, and people involved the manipulation of political traditions which all had their own long histories. Thus, although there was almost limitless innovation, the discourse of traditionalism invited the emulation of many recurrent forms and arrangements. This produced much of the same "invented tradition" language about the restoration of authority and order as we find in Egypt.

Royal language tells us much about not only ideals but also shortcomings and practical politics. As my co-author points out, there are ineluctable distinctions to be made between the official historical accounts written by central states – in rhetoric simulating a world of total and frictionless authority – and the realities of governance, which demanded a politics of negotiation: political buy-in, compliance, and persuasion. The "command rhetoric" used by Mesopotamian kings in their narratives, as in Egypt, was designed to suggest that they exercised complete control over virtually all aspects of state capacity (in warfare, religion, production, knowledge, etc.). But this is deceptive of both fact and even voice. The voice of certainty deliberately obscured not only matters of fact but also the mechanics that made kingdoms function. There is therefore a comparison to be made not just between fiction and fact when reading royal literature, but also between the totalizing ideologies of states and the realities of delegation, power-sharing, and elite settlements. Royal literature routinely magnified the authority of individual rulers to the purpose of symbolically investing a discourse of state functionality in the sole figure of the king as an ideal person. But these symbolic absolutes, reified at the state center, were in reality at variance with the tools and roles of everyday governance which were (necessarily) distributed spatially and socio-politically. It must interest us not only that these major disparities existed but also why this was so consistently the case.

Some of the most durable aspects of the organization of power are in evidence, then, not where the king commanded and his state obeyed, but where the Crown as an institution had to negotiate with temples, civic bodies,[5] and merchants in order to effect its authority. We tend to think of such groups as if royal power was held over them de jure, but it is better to think in terms of the integration, co-option, or de facto recognition by states of the pre-existing authorities of other power-holders. The management of "elites"[6] involved the delicate art of balancing entrenched local networks with meritocracies (both "closed-rank" and "open-rank" systems); controlling competition within and between bureaus and centers; harnessing and crosschecking the flow of information and intelligence from different administrative units through separate chains of command; both permitting and restraining independent action; and, of course, maintaining accountability. To these purposes, there were many tools in the Crown's toolkit: offices and concessions to confer and take away; tax obligations to impose or remit; whole fields of activity to regulate, from animal-skinning to gold-smithing to legal practice; and, of course, the state's recourse of "legitimate" violence.

Meantime, elite groups had their own internal dynamics of power to navigate: maintaining systems of patronage,[7] nepotism, and inherited position; expanding power through intermarriage and business alliances; buttressing social authority

---

[5] See Barjamovic 2004.
[6] By "elites," I mean people holding larger-than-average shares of social and economic power.
[7] Westbrook 2005.

through displays of wealth and prestige. There was the matter of working out pecking orders between elites whose power was based in different institutions. Would a royal tax-collector outrank a city judge in a dispute? Was a priest superior to a mayor? Who would decide? Such things were not spelled out in black and white. There were subtle shades of social surveillance to define and maintain elite status and individual reputation; to police in-group coherence without succumbing to excessive gossip, jealousy, or denunciation. And colonized elites had to balance the authenticity that underwrote their local authority (as judges, priests, mayors, etc.) with duties to the (non-local) political center which could require them to act publicly against the local interests they supposedly represented.

This then raises the question of how autonomous of states were any of the significant political actors or sectors. It is clear that there were always some resources, people, and spheres of activity – and therefore some politics – which lay outside of state control; the question is only how much of this activity is visible to us. The OB was not the first period in which non-state activity is attested, but it is perhaps the first with plentiful evidence in the form of letters, sales, and loans, although in some cases apparently, private merchants worked in tandem with palaces to resell state resources.[8] Thus we see not a sharp divide between Babylonian state and non-state sectors, but two arenas of overlapping action. By contrast, to the north in the contemporaneous Old Assyrian period, a centuries-long overland trade between the city of Aššur and trade colonies in Anatolia shows us a more emphatic dichotomy of state/private activity.

What really makes the OB stand out is not only the explosion of legal contracts forming the core apparatus of private business, but also the distinct cultures of householders, businessmen, and officials that emerge in the voice of their letters, where nonstate competition was worked out. There can be little dispute as to the self-awareness and existence of this group: As in Egypt, it entailed the management of households whose members ranged from *pater familias* down to the sheep; a robust epistolary community; and a terminology of status interaction, including the "influential" (*kabtu*), "gentleman" (*awīlum*), "servant" (*ṣuḫaru*), the "great" and the "small" (*rabû* and *ṣiḫru*), all knit together by a language of friendship, fraternity, and favor. In their letters, we can see class identities being developed and worked out, often with much squabbling.

Social power was perennially under revision, horizontally as much as vertically. Networks of social and economic power existed outside of the state sphere, and this generated its own kind of politics. But this hardly means that

---

[8] See Garfinkle 2007 and von Dassow 2012.

elite identity was secure, stable, or teleologically emergent toward success (quite the contrary: a class of "businessmen" does not re-emerge until the first millennium). I am struck by the difference here with the Egyptian case: The collective elite identity so confidently on display in the *Tale of Sinuhe* cannot be summoned forth from the Mesopotamian literary landscape. Elite identity was very real for individuals, but it remained highly atomistic in political terms, and not part of a "common culture."

Two spatial features both empowered and constrained palatial estates as political institutions trying to emerge into states: concentrated urban nodes and a territorially diffused wealth of arable land. The combination of cities – dynamic social and economic engines – and a nearly limitless amount of agriculturally productive countryside – making "pockets of power" possible almost everywhere in the alluvium – provided kings with unparalleled resources with which to build state power. However, the same conditions permitted a ubiquity of competitors to and emulators of state form and function to flourish, from institutions to individuals. These power constraints acted politically, symbolically, and infrastructurally. It is with this sense of interaction at and between different scales that I go forward to think about power's spatial and social organization, and with some sympathy for states: As in any culture, there was enough competition and comparison at all levels of state society as to make the Crown's task of "organizing" it a plate-spinning act from beginning to end.

2.3 The Cities

From the earliest point when we can identify political entities in Mesopotamia and in every period going forward, they were based in cities. The historical states that ruled the lower alluvium were without exception urban kingships. It is almost impossible to overstate the role of cities in the configuration of social, political, and economic power. Indeed, when Uruk's urban magnitude sprawled across the meadows and marshlands of southern Iraq in the mid-fourth millennium BC, we have no clear evidence of kings or palaces; as far as we can see, there were cities before there were states. But there were temples, and these had priests, officers, staff, dependents, grain reserves, and land, not to mention ideological power and control over the writing technology by which these assets are known to us. It is likely that these temples had some political authority over at least part of the urban community. Urban form and culture would remain the most durable elements of the political landscape, more durable even than dynasties themselves. The city of Uruk, for instance, would outlive not only the five local dynasties that sporadically ruled from it between ca. 2600–1800

BC, but another dozen other states that laid claim to it through the millennia. As a rule, cities both preexisted and outlived kingships.

But if cities were durable, they were also highly protean. If Mesopotamian urbanism was "bigger" than its Egyptian counterpart, it was also more volatile. Cities could attain vast sizes and then shrink back to much smaller footprints. The same city names endured, but the political primacy of one city could be easily replaced by another. For instance, the city of Lagaš in the third millennium was an unrivaled power; by the first millennium, it was barely remembered. Akkad's unification of lower Mesopotamia in the 24th century BC was a feat that kings tried to emulate for centuries, but soon after the dynasty's demise, Akkad was abandoned and referenced only by historical tales and antiquarian restoration projects. Babylon's first dynasty began around 1890 BC, ruled lower Mesopotamia by 1750 BC, and then became the preeminent city of the region for the next 1,500 years; yet we are not even sure it existed before 2000 BC. Thus, though we recognize that cities were engines of social, economic, and political power, and some showed incredible resilience, their political preeminence could be ephemeral.

The symbolic preeminence and relative predominance of cities can also distract us from their variability over time. Mesopotamian cities were much smaller across the second and into the early first millennium than they had been in the third millennium. It is also worth remembering that the majority of Babylonians in all periods did not live in cities; our impression that this was an urban culture is largely shaped by the fact that virtually all of our sources come from cities. If Babylonian cities seem therefore not so "elusive" as their Egyptian counterparts, they also run the risk of overdetermining how we tell the story of Mesopotamian social power.[9]

Still, cities were the centers from which much rural production was administered, on which markets were focused, and where political, religious, and cultural forms and tastes took shape. This leads us to focus on the activities of the administrators, scribes, and businessmen whose names populate the cuneiform contracts, letters, and literature, all drafted, archived, and found in cities. For example, one thinks of successful OB long-distance traders like Ea-nāṣir of Ur, bringing copper ingots across the Persian Gulf; merchants like Šēp-Sîn, who in his letters arranged orders for tin, juniper, and aromatics, running business from Larsa to faraway Susa and collecting kilo upon kilo of silver;[10] or the slavers and wine importers working northern Syria and the Diyala from the Sippar *kārum* ("market district"). There were the high administrators working locally, assigning farmland and converting in-kind taxes into durable silver for

---

[9] See Richardson 2007. [10] See e.g., AbB 9 112 and 134, 12 78, and 13 31.

the states: Balmunamḫe in Larsa, Šamaš-ḫazir in Jaḫrurum-šaplum, and Utul-Ištar in Sippar and Babylon. And there were the learned (as opposed to, say, administrative or military) scribes, such as Sin-nada of 19th-century Ur, training students in his house on everything from elementary texts to Sumerian laments; Nabi-Enlil of 18th-century Nippur, boasting of the superiority of scribal training in his city; or Ipiq-Aya of Sippar of 17th-century Sippar, copying lexical lists, *Atra-ḫasis*, and *Naram-Sin and the Enemy Hordes*.[11] In these same historical milieux, we find other men bearing a dizzying array of state titles such as estate "farmer" ($ensi_2$), tax-collector (šu.i), overseer of merchants (ugula dam.gar_3), and herd supervisor (sipa); civic titles like head of assembly (gal. ukkin.na), mayor (*ḫazannu*), and headman (*rabiānu*); temple titles such as high priest (sanga), administrator ($ša_3$.tam), and cleric ($gudu_4$); and military ranks such as general (ugula mar.tu), captain (nu.$banda_3$), and colonel (PA.PA) – among many others. Some of these offices were sinecures or prebends, with designated incomes or rights-to-collect attached to them; some were assigned by merit or inherited.

But many wealthy householders carried out their business without any titles at all – simply called so-and-so, son of so-and-so – private actors without institutional identity or authority. Often, roles depended on the needs of the moment: OB society was one in which flexibility between private and institutional roles were central to how things worked. Also significant: There is much evidence for the collective rights, properties, and obligations of professional and official *groups* – merchants, soldiers, judges, plantation managers, votaresses, farmers, diviners; occupational classes like bakers, carpenters, millers, and basketmakers; and communities of ethnic, foreign, or metic residents (Isinites, Kassites, Elamites). Most of these individuals and groups, with identities autonomous of states, were documented in cities. Anything like "class consciousness" was at best incipient and inchoate, but what group identities there were, semi-independent of state authority, were all realized in urban venues of decision-making: in city assemblies, collegia of judges, district councils, city wards, temple courts, the "cloisters" in which votary women lived, and harbor districts. All these bodies exercised some internal legal and administrative powers over their members and properties.

These powers were never neatly or clearly "nested" *à la* Weber within rational structures of state law and administration. So we are left with a terribly messy picture of "how power worked," because the combination or bases of authority behind decisions seem as numerous and protean as the actors. The same kinds of functions could be performed by different officials in

---

[11] See Van Koppen 2011.

different ways, with little obvious reason for doing things differently. To take but a single (but significant) example, the measurement of fields, important for ownership and taxation, is known to have been performed by (among others): surveyors (*abi ašli*), clerks (šà.tam), accountants (sag.du$_5$), "gentlemen" (*awīlū*), city elders (*šib ālim*), the "old men" (*awīlū lābirutê*), military scribes (dub.sar zag.ga), supervisors (*šāpirū*), administrators (*rābiṣū*), judges (di.ku$_5$), military governors (*šakkanakkū*), and captains (PA.PA).[12] It is never made clear why certain officers rather than others were called on to perform this specific action. In many cases, not only did more than one type of official preside over acts of measuring, but it was done under the "supervision" of a (non-human) divine emblem.

If one takes field-measuring and extends it as a metaphor for other types of governmental or collective action – judging, taxing, mobilizing manpower, maintenance of infrastructure, and so on – it seems simply impossible to draw a coherent flow-chart of power. I do not mean to imply that sense and order cannot be found: often enough, judging was done by judges, messages were brought by messengers, and city matters were deliberated by assemblies. I mean to say that governance was not only handled heterogeneously, but also that Mesopotamians themselves rarely expressed the idea that any particular officer was exclusively appropriate to perform any particular task.

One way we might make sense of this seemingly chaotic picture is to try to understand the system's complexity as its virtue; to see what is seemingly asystematic as … flexible. What Mesopotamian state society displays is a laboratory in which a diversity of resources and infrastructural powers allowed equally diverse pathways for the allocation of labor, resources, and talent. A wide array of actors and institutions permitted and diffused the inevitable pressures of ambition and competition. Institutions limited risk and overuse, and regulated community goods; private households allowed for the realization of opportunities; and both interacted in the same markets and other public arenas. This environment of complexity never emerged or resolved toward any perfect equilibrium – many letters tell us how often ambitions were thwarted, resources were wasted, officials quarreled, and power was misused – but it arguably created systemic resilience. And indeed those same letters are suffused with expectations that these things *should* work: if only person X hadn't been greedy, or person Y so lazy, everything would have worked out fine. These potentialities, hopes, and ambitions that urban elites had for stability were real, even if problems and failures are better attested in the record. It is the existence of *expectations* that gives more reasonable testimony for the "organization of power" than their

---

[12] See Richardson 2020, 225–226, 237–238.

satisfaction. Mesopotamian cities were, in their most abstract sense, the formal expression of a *desire* for order, places where one could hope to find "truth and justice" (*kitti u mīšari*), while the dangerous and disordered world outside the city walls – in the steppes, meadows, and mountains – was kept at bay. It is not only that cities were where one might to find power; cities were the only places where organization was possible.

2.4 Provinces and the Territorialized State

Because cities were such dominant communities, the provincialization of Mesopotamia emerged only slowly. Areal units never really took on the conceptual importance that nodal cities had, as the denomination of territory makes clear. From the earliest writings of the Uruk period, we can reconstruct a toponymic repertoire composed entirely of city names and devoid of regional ones (as far as we can read them; see Bauer et al. 1998: 92–94). It was not until the Early Dynastic period – not earlier than ca. 2500 BC – that any city controlled enough land to require specific names for ex-urban territory or terms for boundaries.[13] Only one royal inscription from this time describes anything like a systematic provincialization of territory. Giša-kidu of Umma (ca. 2400 BC) described the frontier of his state as it was supposedly given on an already-existing "monument of the god Šara":

> From the Āl-[x] canal to the Dua-canal is 45 nindan ...
> from the Dua-canal to the ... is x nindan ...
> from [x] to the fortress Dūr-gara is 21,630 nindan ...
> from the fortress Dūr-gara to Nag-nanše is 636 nindan ...
> ... he did not go beyond its levee ...[14]

The breaks in the text do not permit a full reconstruction of the boundaries Giša-kidu describes, but the perimeter may have been something like 67 kilometers, giving us an area for the Umma state of about 357 km².[15] What is remarkable is not so much the information given by such an inscription, but that no other king would offer any similar "cadastral" description of his state for another 300 years.[16] Simply put, where kings were interested in conveying geographic information, it was overwhelmingly about loci that had been conquered, not areas under control.

---

[13] Notably the ki-sur boundary for the Gu'edena (lit., "edge-of-the-steppe") field, as early as Eanatum.

[14] RIME 1 12.6.2: 26–78.

[15] Steinkeller (2017: 564) estimated that 102 km² of Umma territory was Crown land in the Ur III period. The city occupied ca. 2% of that area, ca. = 2.25 km².

[16] Until Ur-Namma of Ur, ca. 2100 BC: RIME 3/2 1.1.21, with more toponyms but fewer specific (or plausible) dimensions.

The process of formal territorialization was not much advanced in the Akkadian dynasty. Under Sargon of Akkad and his successors, a few parts of the state were named for the individual people, elite households, and cities that controlled them, rather than as toponyms in their own right. However, despite this dearth of areal nomenclature, Akkadian state practices do show a sense of territorial awareness: large tracts of land were routinely reassigned from one city to another, new administrative units were created far from city centers, and the titles of some urban grandees were recoded to mean something less like "city lord" and more like "provincial governor." Notwithstanding, when an enormous revolt was organized against the Akkadian state, the leaders of the uprising were all called kings of cities and not heads of provinces; the centers of power remained firmly urban.

In later Mesopotamian states, there was more emphasis on the organization of territory into provinces, but the process never really came to completion. In Ur III times, the land was organized under "governors" ($ensi_2$) and "generals" (šagina) appointed to cities, and peripheral conquered areas were termed "the lands" (ma-da). That the cities could be understood as the "capitals" of whole provinces is suggested by the structure of the formerly independent state of Lagaš, which was now divided into three districts (Girsu, Lagaš, and the gu_2-ab-ba, lit. "bank of the sea"). For a period of about half a century, deliveries of in-kind goods and livestock to the state (in Sumerian called bala, lit., a "turn[ing]") were organized by province, but the role of provinces is somewhat obscured by the fact that the governors delivered but sometimes also received bala-payments. It is thus not clear whether the provincial system enabled what was fundamentally a "tax" paid to a center, a structure of entitlements for elite persons, or a redistributive arrangement benefiting the cultic economy of the city temples rather than for provinces as such.[17]

In the OB period, the evidence for territorial administration is even less regular. This is unsurprising given the division of the alluvium between multiple warring city-states with differing governance and accounting systems. But we do get some glimpses of territorial administration. The documents of the Larsa state, for instance, show that enormous tracts of agricultural lands were organized under its authority. Hammurabi's Babylonian state divided its southern territory into "lower" (šaplûm[18]) and "upper" (an.ta) regions and recognized other regional districts (ḫalṣum).[19] Some "governors" (šāpirū and gir_3.$nita_2$) presided over cities (Sippar, Kiš, Dilbat, Rapiqum, etc.), but others over terminologically indistinct (but nevertheless specific) regions called "the lands"

---

[17] See Sharlach 2004 and Dahl 2006; cf. Yoffee 1998 on OB cultic economy.
[18] Charpin et al. 2004: 83–84 n. 290; cf. Charpin 1981.
[19] E.g., the ḫalṣums for Suḫum and Jamutbal. See AbB 14 132, distinguishing a town (ālum) from its province (ḫalṣum).

and "the river district." The greatest amount of textual specificity about production and taxation, however, was still produced at the city level, where local watering districts (*ugārū*) were responsible for payment of taxes and corvée labor, even down to the individual level as specified in field-rental contracts. Rural lands were represented as administrative categories from an urban perspective, not neutral geographic facts. Thus, city identities remained at the fore while regional-provincial ones were always relatively weak.

Provincialization increased in the Kassite and Middle Babylonian periods, when as many as fifteen provinces (*piḥatū*) were administered by a central government at Babylon through governors called *šandabakkū*.[20] This may reflect the long period of low urbanization from the Middle Bronze through Iron II period – more a sign of weak cities than of strong provincial identities. The administration of the city-province of Nippur is well known, but its texts constitute about 90 percent of all documentation for the period, most from only about half the time span of the dynasty (ca. 1360–1225 BC), so it is unclear how representative the corpus is. Some lands remained under the direct administration of the king and semi-independent grandees called "manor lords" (*bēl bīti*, lit. "master of households"), but it is unclear if these estates were really "provinces." Notwithstanding, a larger number of territories were now named for tribes or regions rather than cities, and this seems to reflect state structure as more regionally defined.

Despite the low profile of provincialization, the lands were important to states: The majority of people and productive wealth in Babylonia in all periods were in rural territory rather than in cities. Nor did cities administer all the territory in their hinterlands – beyond their immediate arable fields and second-/third-tier villages lay vast swaths of unorganized land.[21] In virtually all periods, our texts mention places that could not have been much further than the farming villages under urban administration but were clearly not directly exploited. We know these places existed, but we cannot say much about them. In effect, the enormous substrate land wealth that lay outside the scope of states remains hidden from us. This again reflects on state ontology. The absence of provincial identities and the preponderance of urban power reflects just how referential the state project really was: states documented what they administered, not everything that existed. Babylonian state ideology was content to sound as if it governed all the places or nodes that "counted" – that is, that kings held kingship over a collection of individual cities rather than over a single, unified "land." But we should avoid thinking that what was left unexplained was unimportant.

---

[20] Cf. OB gu₂.en.na, "governor" (of Nippur).   [21] See Liverani 1996 and 1999.

Structurally, Babylonia as a "state" thus perennially appears to have been a galaxy of cities with orbital towns; beyond and between, there was unadministered interstitial territory which was never clearly demarcated or denominated. How "provincialized" Mesopotamian states were may depend on whether one interprets the administrative divisions named for cities as implicating (some? most? all?) of their associated ex-urban territories. But at no point was a single system to organize all state land into administrative units either achieved or sought. In contrast to a retrospective reconstruction of territoriality in the Egyptian case, the hard evidence for administration by territory in Mesopotamia remains wanting, despite our modern analytic preferences to define states (ancient and otherwise) as structured on familiar principles of regularly divided land.

The corollary is that the constraint which limited kingship as an urban institution also kept in check the ambitions of local elites who might have tried to establish provincial power bases, as they sometimes could do in Egypt. As much as Babylonian states were unsuccessful at creating isomorphic spatial entities called "provinces," setting a lower boundary on their power, that same boundary fixed a ceiling on the aspirations of governors and city lords. It remained difficult for local peers, powerful though they might be in local towns, to cobble together clear, heritable, and reproducible political identities in the same way states could. Until the Neo-Babylonian period, elites were not a class with political ambitions (in either the Marxist or Weberian sense), a coherent cultural habitus (Bourdieu), or "autonomous" of imperial power (Eisenstadt). And to the extent that they did achieve such definition and consciousness, they remained rooted in cities, not in provinces. The elite networks of power that undergirded the historical states superimposed on Babylonia's landscape were not based on regional or provincial identities.

2.5 Cities and Their Others

Although kingship was a fundamentally urban form of power, cities themselves were semi-autonomous of royal power. Moreno García's observation that Egyptian cities grew in the early second millennium as older crown centers were abandoned (see p. 50) excites an important question on the Mesopotamian side: given the centrality of royal authority and cities to Mesopotamian political power, why were they so uneasily integrated into one another? Kings styled themselves as kings of specific cities (Ur, Akkad, Ur again, Babylon) and their main palaces were built there, but the cities were not "theirs"; they did not, as a rule, found or own those cities, acts which were prerogatives of the gods. Babylonian kings founded all kinds of new settlements, often eponymously named, as "fortresses" and "harbors" – purpose-built military and trade centers – but these were generally not capital cities. For instance, Paul-Alain Beaulieu (2017: 7) writes of a new Kassite royal city, "there is no evidence that the Kassite rulers intended to replace Babylon with Dūr-Kurigalzu as capital of their kingdom. Indeed, they continued to claim the title of 'king of Babylon'." Conversely, although many Babylonian cities developed kingship traditions,[22] others never claimed to be the centers of royal states at all, or only briefly flirted with ephemeral local kingships: Fara, Abu Ṣalabikh, Zabalam, Nippur, Sippar, and so on, even when they were economically or ideologically important.[23]

This underscores a fundamental distinction between kingship and cities as distinct loci of political power. Babylonian kingship was an inextricably urban form and yet unable to independently reproduce itself *as* that form, whereas cities could carry on, autonomously and quite successfully, without needing to assert or brand their identity with dynastic kingship. Even the etiological *Sumerian King List*, profoundly inaccurate in factual terms, correctly acknowledges this difference through its narrative structure: cities pre-existed (and survived) kingship – beginning as it does: "When kingship descended from heaven, the kingship was in Eridu ... " – but kingships were transient and very mortal. This principle is exemplified in Sumerian city laments, which make clear that kingship was *dependent* on the well-being of tutelary gods and the patronized cities.

I will return to discuss non-royal city institutions: wards, assemblies, merchants, temples, cloisters, guilds, and so on. But first I will make a distinction of royal from urban power on territorial grounds, to give a sense of the nonurban settlements founded and funded by the Crown. If the Crown built few cities, it did build other kinds of places – fortresses, storage-and-distribution centers, palace-(town)s, manors, military colonies, brick-firing plants, caravanserais, and threshing centers. The social lives of these places are nowhere nearly as well-studied (or, admittedly, represented by evidence) as proper cities, but they provide nevertheless a glimpse of nonurban state power.

In the Early Dynastic period, royal building work was almost exclusively within cities; nonurban royal settlements are sparsely attested.[24] But the Akkadian kings made extensive use of redistricting and purchases to carve off some productive hinterlands from city control, appointing new governors and

---

[22] Including Lagaš, Kiš, Uruk, Umma, Adab, Akkad, Ur, Isin, Larsa, Babylon, Ešnunna, Mananā, Malgium, Der, Diniktum, a.o., some of them in multiple dynastic iterations.

[23] The Sumerian King List lists dynasties for four cities with no evidence for kingship (Šuruppak, Eridu, Bad-Tibira, and Larag).

[24] Pre-Akkadian references to fortresses include RIME 1 9.5.27, 12.6.2; to palaces, 9.5.23 and .27; 9.9.2 and .6; to manorial estates, perhaps 9.5.17(?).

deploying gangs of workers in the countryside. Few nonurban places were ever mentioned in the royal inscriptions of the Akkadian kings, but we can see that a great deal of administrative energy was focused there.

The ensuing Ur III period saw the Crown's construction of distribution centers like Puzriš-Dagan and agricultural estates like Garšana (see Owen ed. 2010). The Old Babylonian period provides sources for fortresses as diverse as Ḫaradum, a small desert fort on the middle-Euphrates with a modest civic life, and Dūr-Abi-ešuḫ, a multi-site complex that cycled equipment, provisions, and troops to and from other fortresses. The names of many fortresses are evocative of loyalism ("Fort {Royal Name}" was a common form), military ethos ("Claw of the God"; "Circle Fort"; "Watchpost"), and rural location ("Sandbank"; "Ox-Drover-Town"). Larsa in the Old Babylonian period and the *narû*-monuments of the Kassite period attest to the vibrant life of "manors," the towns of powerful individuals who ruled them as personal domains. Many such places were simply called Āl-PN, "Town of so-and-so." Thus, although Babylonian kings ruled as city lords through patronage and protection, they exercised more direct power outside of cities, where they acted as the masters of estates. This model is heuristically useful, allowing us to understand that every king was simultaneously a king of different places in different ways. It also hints at how royal power was perpetually constrained by the institutional power of socioeconomic elites in cities on the one hand and the diffusion of territorial power in a larger number of smaller places of the countryside. Babylonian royal power was a balancing act between these two realms of governance (or: "governmentalities"). We are looking not so much at a "two-sector" state as we are at two different kinds of kingship operating simultaneously.

We know much less of the many rural places and populations outside of royal emplacements: in trading posts, farming towns, and herding camps. These were little places that looked to towns rather than cities as their central places; where no state officer was stationed, no Crown property documented, and no taxes paid. No account of the "organization of power" could be complete without modeling these "unorganized" communities or the chieftains and elders who ran them (Selz 2010). We know these places were out there based on often single mentions in state texts: border towns, lonely farmsteads, and fishing camps; sheepfolds in the meadowlands, *mudhifs* in the marshes, watchtowers in the steppe; and Kassite outfits, Elamite camps, a "region of the tents." One OB letter mentions a dispute adjudicated by city judges in a village called Laliya, which had a mayor and village elders (AbB IX 268); another mentions an expensive field located in Bitutu (AbB II 114); and a third orders a worker from Tell-Ištazri to report for duty at the palace gate (AbB II 17). None of these three places is mentioned in any other cuneiform text, but well-known enough for the letter-writers not to have to specify their location. But where were these places? How were they related to nearby states? Were they under their control, barely known, or torn between states? We cannot know. The problem is not small: most OB toponyms are attested only a few times. The relationship between poorly attested toponyms and state centers remains an intriguing macro-level historical question; our continued focus on better-attested places obscures how extensive undocumented toponyms really are.

Urban states and their associated settlements might thus be represented as flickers of light in a vast, dark space, where only a portion of the landscape was illuminated by the symbols and actors who made state power apparent. Another kind of power pertained in other places – the Places Where the State Was Not – a great "unorganized" part of the landscape that minimized its interactions with the rapacious men who styled themselves "kings" in sometimes nearby towns; an ancient lifeway not defined by kingship or cities.

If life outside of state society was actually the more typical experience for any given Babylonian person, this casts a different light on state claims. Take for example the repeated declarations of OB kings to have "gathered in the scattered people" and "settled them in peaceful abodes." Given that few kings claimed control over territory (rather, over peer cities) – it seems likely that these in-gatherings were not forced population movements, but attempts to persuade, recruit, and maintain political clientele. Some significant portion of the rural population belonged to different states at different times; others remained unaligned with any state. There seems always to have been a broad and entropic landscape ready to absorb populations back into (as it must have appeared from the perspective of state ontology) a non-state "nothingness." This unexpectedly inspires some sympathy for states: Their claims to control people were not confident, factual descriptions, but desperate attempts to sound as if this control might become real.

Non-state populations, whether they posed security risks or unrealized sources of income for states, were of varying importance across Mesopotamian history. Although cities were dominant in all periods, their size and number, relative to other kinds of settlements, varied dramatically from century to century. In the Early Dynastic period, 88 percent of the occupational area surveyed was located in settlements 100 hectares or larger: a thoroughly urbanized population. By the Kassite period, sites of this size made up only about 31 percent of all settled areas: a thoroughly ruralized population. Cities only returned as a majority form by the Neo-Babylonian period (Adams 1981). There was also regional variation within periods. For instance, the region around Nippur perennially had more than twice as many small villages (2 ha. or less) as Uruk (Richardson 2007: 16). There was thus wide variation in the urban:rural populations from time to time and place to place. Accordingly, different cities had sometimes widely disparate experiences trying to regulate their control of hinterlands.

States we might think of as basically similar illustrate this variability. The OB kingdoms of Larsa and Babylon, for instance, were contemporary rivals and near-equals in terms of political and military power. But Larsa harnessed vast productive areas in its hinterlands: from Bad-Tibira in the west to Lagaš in the east, hundreds of surveyed fields were annually plowed, planted, and harvested in dozens of agricultural towns and estates. The kingdom had at least 8,223 hectares (82.2 km²) of arable land under state production in any given year; one single account text from Larsa (YBC 7238) alone documents more than 1,200 hectares of farmland. Babylon, by contrast, had a radically lower footprint in its rural hinterlands: despite a similar density of text types, the largest single register from Sippar (the best documented of Babylon's subject cities) accounts for only 222.9 hectares of land (MHET II 6 894), a sixth the size of the land in the YBC 7238 account. The kingdom of Larsa appeared to exercise more power over a wider area than Babylon did; its officials, resources, administrative apparatus, encumbered persons, tax yields, and so on, reflect this.

In all periods, cities were centers of administration, organizing and exploiting agricultural wealth. Mesopotamian state power was always a mediation between centers and distributed bases of wealth. But wide variations in practice by period and area inflected the nature of rule in individual states, with results as diverse as the royal work camps of the Akkadian period, the state-run redistribution system of the Ur III bala, and the decentered manorial system of the Kassite period. Small differences of degree in the algorithms of production resulted in political-economic forms that were substantially different in kind.

2.6 Semi- and Informal Networks of Power

There were other networks of power-holders partly or wholly based in cities whose affinities did not lie primarily with state. The interests of local officials, family lineages, private households, and temple communities sometimes intersected or overlapped with those of royal households, but sometimes diverged from them. Competing cadres of officers, private entrepreneurs with goods to protect from taxation, and priests with prebends to pass on within their families all had assets worth withholding from state control.

One might object that "officers" do not belong on this list – that their very institutional titles mean they did not belong to "informal" networks. But titles were often given in de-facto recognition of an individual's already-existing private economic and social power. Officials often bore titles that had little to do with the actual functions they performed. This is a well-known problem in Assyriology: "fishermen" sometimes turn out to be soldiers, "farmers" were county supervisors, "barbers" and "inn-keepers" were tax-collectors, "temple sweepers" and "shepherds" were only the supervisors of men who did the actual work, and the "Great One of the Assembly" was responsible for mobilizing field labor. The royal official called a *rakbû* appears most often as a messenger, but is also attested witnessing sales, collecting barley, and receiving taxes. Officials called "Overseers of the Merchants" dealt with credit and financing, but also acted as judges and transacted their own personal business. The responsibilities of officials to one another appear to be haphazardly individual and occasional, by title, type of action, and city. We cannot therefore always be certain whether in any given instance an official was acting in his capacity *as* an official, as a private person merely noted by/with his title, or whether titles inherently conferred broad powers to act in ways beyond what the titles described.

An example: Sin-nādin-šumi was a 17th century "diviner" (*barû*) by title and a servant of the King of Babylon. But his dozens of texts documenting activities over approximately twenty-five years have little to do with either divination or royal service. He mostly extended short-term loans of silver and grain and provided cultic sheep to the Šamaš temple in Sippar. He built up a regular circle of contract witnesses and partners as his personal business associates. He lived as a local grandee in the fortress town of Kullizu ("Ox-Drover Town"), and not as a functionary in a large city. This "official" was much more a financier and sometime state/temple factor than a mantic ritualist.[25]

Of course, sometimes titles are clearly related to area of responsibility. Šamaš-ḫāzir, for instance, was the "registrar" (sag-dun$_3$) for the farmlands of the conquered Larsa province; accordingly, he made field assignments to tenant farmers. Utu-šumundab, the "Overseer of the Merchants" at Sippar, mostly arranged credit sales to convert crops into taxable silver. City elders deliberated in the assemblies, judges judged, and tax-collectors assessed the dues owed on fields. Sometimes people did exactly what their job titles describe.

But even when we have a clear picture of what officials were supposed to do, it can be hard to understand how their job worked within an administrative *system*. There are few titles for which we can establish clear chains of command, either within or between branches of civil, military, or institutional administration. It can therefore be hard to say who anyone reported to, on whose authority they acted, or to whom the silver they collected would get kicked up. Nor can we in most cases know how or why people were selected as officeholders in the first place. Their first appearance in a text *as* an official is typically the first time they

---

[25] See further Richardson 2010: 58–69.

are attested at all; officials thus seem to materialize out of thin air. Career promotion is likewise difficult to track. We can point to a few instances in which a specific individual held first one title and then another. From the Late OB, the best-known cases are those of Utu-šumundab and Utul-Ištar, who were titled judge and scribe (respectively) in the 1640s, and then identified as Overseer of Merchants and Foreman of the Workers in the 1630s. But we do not know the reason for the title changes. One is left to assume these were promotions, but even this is unclear. As isolated cases, they cannot be held up as models of any tenure-track system.

However, states were successful at grafting a stratum of officialdom onto the class of landholders and merchants who were truly at the core of OB society. Official positions were really not specific jobs with specific duties answerable to a specific bureaucracy; they de facto identified individuals as palace clients, scattered throughout the kingdom and acting as royal agents on an as-needed basis, with broad latitude to act. While state businesses relied on authority delegated to them, their agency was used to build relationships and manage resources for their own personal affairs. This required local political alliances and business contacts in various sectors of the economy: in production, transport, storage, finance, and so on. One might better think of Babylonian officials as *concessionaires*, men – and they were almost always men – holding grants to command and collect, with basic obligations to deliver annual quotas of wealth to the state center.

This environment led to local networks of officials who worked to meet Crown demands for taxes.[26] Some of these networks were formalized, such as judges *in collegium* (di.ku$_5$.meš) or merchants incorporated as the *kārum*. Other groups were ad hoc, only visible to us when we can identify the repeated appearance of specific people in separate texts. These networks had clear advantages in that states did not need to invest much financial or political capital in running *systems* of government: granted titles were incentive enough. Officials, meanwhile, were free to operate as they liked through their "circle of acquaintances."[27] The disadvantages, unsurprisingly, came when individuals used offices for personal gain and where official cliques formed, leading to competition and conflict. The delegation of authority was a slippery slope; as Moreno García felicitously puts it, it created a spectrum of administrative ethos ranging from "collaboration, negotiation, co-opting, favoritism, patronage [to] bribery." The letters between OB officials include mutual accusations of hiding information, stealing money, working behind each other's back, allying with

---

[26] See Mynářová and Alivernini eds. 2020 (esp. Goddeeris, Chambon, DeGraef, and Richardson), and Valk and Soto Marín eds. 2021.

[27] E.g., AbB XIII 78. Old Babylonian letters make frequent reference to what had been "told" and "heard"; clearly a whole informational network existed outside of what was written.

Figure 4 The litigants and various officials adjudicating or intervening in the dispute between Ilšu-ibni and Ipqu-ilīšu the judge mentioned in the Old Babylonian letter AbB XII 2. Disputes between individual officials could entangle whole networks of public and private power. Drawings by Ella Karev.

rivals, snitching, or full-on denunciations to the king (e.g., AbB 12 93). A single lawsuit between individuals, like the one described here between one Ilšu-ibni and a judge named Ipqu-ilīšu, could entangle numerous officers and adjudicating bodies (in boldface; Figure 4):

> Concerning what you wrote to me (**Iluni**), this is what you (**Ilšu-ibni**) said: "**Ipqu-ilīšu the judge** has spoken at length against me in **the assembly**. May a written order be issued that my complaint must be investigated." ... I have spoken to **the gentleman** and I have sent a strongly worded letter on **the gentleman's** behalf for **the director** to **Ipqu-Nabium the barber**, a letter to **Sîn-rēmēni the judge** for his information, and a letter of **the assembly** to **the honorable judges**. Do not spare this **Ipqu-ilīšu** during the litigation in **the assembly**! In accordance with the words that you and he speak against each other in **the assembly**, **the gentlemen** will reprimand **Ipqu-ilīšu the judge**, and they will send me a copy of their tablets. **The gentleman** will inform **the king** according to the litigation that he will hear. (AbB XII 2).[28]

---

[28] In this spirit, see Renger 1973: "Who *Are* All Those People?". Cf. Joannès et al. 2006 no. 31, proceedings against a corrupt mayor.

Other letters about this same dispute vaguely mention a house, an ox, and a field. But we may never know what this quarrel was actually about, partly because the letters are preoccupied with specifying the relations between all the members of this network. The passage outlines a whole chain of prior communications, both extra-textual ("speaking against," "complaint," "investigation," "litigation," "reprimand") and textual (a "written order," "tablets," three other letters, one of them "strongly worded"). None of these letters even hint at what the squabble was about. What we can divine from them is relatively abstract: the range/number of people, offices, and official bodies involved and a density of communications. We can see that nodes of semi-formal power could harden into factions or cliques, and that the affordances of the communicative system were themselves crucial to their creation. From the point of view of states, conflict needed to be channeled and controlled; from the local point of view, a circle of associates might align with a palace while also folding in private commercial, political, and even social goals and grievances.

"Great households" were other sites of power formation. The term encompasses temples or any large establishments exceeding private households in size – with non-family dependents, properties, in-house accounting, and so on. Such organizations probably antedated states and writing altogether; it is not possible to overstate their importance across Mesopotamian history. Temples are our best examples: While serving as a locus for cult and sacrifice, they also provided close to the full portfolio of services that states offered with the possible exception of military defense. Temples were the social and sometimes residential homes for dependents; owned fields, animals, and slaves; ran mills, breweries, brick-making factories, bakeries, and workshops; conferred authority on civic and state proceedings; were staffed by priests, ritualists, gatekeepers, courtyard sweepers, snake-charmers, doctors, and scribes; collected taxes; financed caravans; appointed local notables as prebendiaries; accepted votary personnel into service; organized public labor; provided standards of weights and measures; held repositories of literary and scientific texts – the list could go on.[29] The larger temple communities of Ur III and Neo-Babylonian times commanded memberships and resources rivalling state capacity (Figure 5). While kings routinely laid claim to divine authority and temple patronage, temples were functionally isomorphic to states in many ways, sometimes even forming points of resistance to their authority.

Some collectives belonged to more than one orbit. For example, there were six orders of votary women in the OB whom we rather clumsily call "priestesses"

---

[29] Modern universities are socio-political worlds autonomous of state authority, thus analogous to "great households": with their own legal, financial, membership, and enforcement procedures.

Figure 5 Old Babylonian cuneiform text from Nerebtum listing barley harvested from fields held by sanga-priests. Major temples sometimes held lands and resources rivalling those of the states in which they were situated. ISAC Museum A7641, courtesy of the Institute for the Study of Ancient Cultures of the University of Chicago.

(though we know little of their cultic obligations).[30] We can see that they functioned as entrepreneurs and heads-of-household, with special legal status and sometimes independent residences. These "religious" orders acted as franchises that allowed wealthy families to install daughters into tax-sheltered households from which paternal wealth could be expanded out of the reach of state taxation. Another example: Merchants' collectives had clear obligations to deliver taxes and dues to the Crown, duties of civil administration, and even perform some ad hoc state diplomacy. But they did so by way of their primary local and long-distance trade and finance practices which enriched them as groups and individuals. Thus some classes of persons (metic citizens, soldiers, innkeepers, sailors, and judges) had special responsibilities to institutions, but also corresponding autonomies and privileges.

---

[30] I.e., *kulmašītu*, *nadītu*, *qadištu*, *sekretu*, *šugītu*, and *ugbabtu*.

When it comes to informal networks of power, we may think of natal households as the most "natural" and bedrock form of social relations, with extended families controlling generational wealth. Descent is indeed indicated in Babylonian documents as the core of identity – one was named "So-and-so, *son of So-and-so*" – and some networks were centered on kinship ties. However it is very difficult to reconstruct most Babylonian family trees beyond a three-generation horizon, which seems to reflect the reality of families' ephemeral nature. Indeed, the power of the most important people in OB documents cannot be tied to large families (just as they cannot consistently be tied to titles).

Principles of lineage and dynasticism were not even so clearly at the core of OB kingship as one might think. Although the First Dynasty of Babylon was comprised of a single line of descent over 300 years, the contemporary throne of Larsa was occupied by men from more than a half dozen lineages. Not once in any royal inscription, hymn, or year-name does any of the sixteen kings of the Isin I "dynasty" call himself the son of any previous ruler, even though we know that some were.[31] Descent and dynasticism were not forefronted ideologically, despite what we might suppose of the importance of lineage to the so-called "Amorite dynasties." Other Mesopotamian states were different: Some Early Dynastic rulers propagated images of their families on plaques[32]; the Ur III royal family was exceptionally extensive; and the Assyrian King List took great pains to confabulate an unbroken line of descent across almost 2,000 years. The role of descent was thus emphasized to different degrees in different periods, but family networks were not always the "natural" sites of power formation that that we might expect them to be.

Important families, however, show up in almost every era. Several prominent families of merchants and landowners are known from Sargonic Nippur. Five generations of the Ur-Meme family held on to a clutch of titles as priests and governors in the same city under the kings of Ur (Figure 6).[33] In the former case, generational wealth proceeded from finance; in the latter, primarily from the incomes attached to prebendiary offices. At OB Sippar, we find prominent families such that of as Ilšu-ibni, Overseer of the Merchants, with four generations attested holding also judgeships; of Ipiq-Aya, with six generations attested, known as merchants, judges, and scribes mastering literary masterpieces;[34] of lamentation priests such as Inanna-mansum and Ur-Utu,

---

[31] Not even in inscriptions flowery enough to invite such a claim (e.g., RIME 4 1.4.8 or the Laws of Lipit-Ištar) or explicitly retrospective of earlier Isin kings (e.g., RIME 4 1.10.11). Rather, Isin I kings called themselves "sons" of deities. See Charpin et al. 2004: 60–64.

[32] E.g., RIME 1 9.1. 2; Ur-Nanše founded a dynasty at Lagaš, but did not come from one.

[33] See Sallaberger 1999a: 191–193, on the Ur-Meme family. On private enterprise in this period, see Garfinkle 2012; but note that the important Ur III merchant Turam-ilī in forty texts barely mentions his father and no sons.

[34] Van Koppen 2011: esp. 154 for a family tree.

Figure 6 Seal of Lugal-engardu, son of Enlil-amaḫ, prefect of the Inanna temple in Nippur and priest of Enlil (fl. ca. 2050 BC). Lugal-engardu was a third-generation member of the so-called "House of Ur-Meme," a five-generation family which spanned the entire 21st century, perhaps outlasting even the Ur III dynasty itself. Members of this family held titles as scribes, provincial governors, and priests. ISAC Museum A31067, courtesy of the Institute for the Study of Ancient Cultures of the University of Chicago.

with up to seven generations known, with significant interests in landholding, beer brewing, and the cultic economy of sacrifice. Some actors, such as some *nadītu*-women, accrued enough wealth to split away from their paternal households and begin their own lines of inheritance. The role of families seems to have grown in later periods. For instance, a majority of economic activity documented at 6th-century Uruk (once again a large city of ca. 12,500 persons) can be connected to about six dozen families,[35] and hundreds of texts from 5th-century Nippur detail the business of the wealthy Murašû family, with interests in landowning and finance.

An important question for the study of ancient Mesopotamian families has been the extent to which kinship relations formed the basis for the accrual and generational transfer of wealth in state societies. Opinions diverged after

---

[35] Van De Mieroop 1997: 107–108 and nn. 13–14; in his opinion, "a merging of extended family and professional ties."

a proposition by Soviet scholars that families lay behind most Mesopotamian economic and social formations. No clear answer ever emerged from this debate,[36] but it is undeniable that kinship structures played important roles in some times and places. For OB times, this has been studied in detail at Ur, at Nippur, and at Sippar, with especially clear results for the concentration of landholding, titles, and professions within single families.

But more important than family in this period was an emerging class identity for the heads of private urban households called *awīlū* – people Robert McC. Adams (2010) called "notables," though I prefer the term "gentlemen." Members of this in-group only sometimes bore titles; membership was not dependent on institutional affiliation. To be recognized as a "gentleman" required some critical mass of social capital from a portfolio of attributes. One must: maintain a fully staffed household, with wife, children, servants, slaves, and large animals; own real property; have proficiency in letter-writing; adhere to behaviors of dress and public comportment; and sustain a public reputation reflecting dependability in private, neighborhood, and business affairs. The importance of reputation is underscored by the fact that the signature activity of this community was the witnessing of contracts. Such men might also command cultural capital: pursuing literary knowledge, making pious votive gifts or private inscriptions, and participating in civic life as judges, assemblymen, or elders. The households of "gentlemen" were the epicenters of class identity and social memory, with documentation of family property extending back as much as a century and the dead buried under the floors.[37] In the epistolary community created by their letters, the "gentlemen" reflect peer social sympathies based on appeals to fraternity, collegiality, and favor. The pathos, anxiety, comparison, and peer pressure of class consciousness is on display; the group was created as much by fear of falling out of status as by being in it.[38]

Perhaps the signature achievement of this emerging class was its recognition under law. Hammurabi's law codex enumerated legal privileges for these *āwīlū*, distinguishing them from other less-favored classes. The perspective of the *āwīlū* also emerges in this first great age of Akkadian literature, with new works putting focus on the problems and perspectives of individuals: Wealth and good fortune were fleeting, peers and neighbors could become competitors instead of allies, and personal gods and individual fates were as important as the great gods accessible only via temple sacrifice. This differed profoundly from the viewpoint of Sumerian literature and its collective, normative *Weltanschauung*. The

---

[36] See Renger 1994. [37] Janssen 2022.
[38] Sallaberger 1999b; Richardson 2022, with literature (esp. sources cited there as De Graef 2008, Janssen 2018, and Jursa and Häckl 2011).

sensibility is also visible in the new omen literature, in which divination was performed for private individuals as well as kings, with potential outcomes related to private concerns about health, wealth, and marriage, and not just statecraft. No fully denominated private "class," autonomous of institutions, ultimately emerged from this era. But the perspective of the private householder remained permanently imprinted on Mesopotamian culture – a "new values and new ethos," as Moreno García puts it. The merchant and householder, as much as the priest and the king, moved into the forefront of social archetypes and would remain there until the last wedge was written.

Tribes and other ethnically denoted groups (with gentilic collective names such as Suteans, Amorites, Kassites, etc.) were another consistent presence in the lower alluvium, sometimes partially integrated into Babylonian urban society.[39] The ethnolinguistic distinction of such people from Babylonians is often unclear. The names are sometimes just administrative designations, demonyms, or exonyms rather than real ethnonyms. Others were disdainful epithets, such as "Gutian" or "Subarian," carrying the sense of "northern mountain person" and no meaningful ethnolinguistic information. We can be sure of linguistic difference in a few cases, as with Hurrians; but then we find no interest on the part of Babylonians to give "Hurrians" a group name as such.[40] Conversely, the common ethnonym "Elamite" denoted a broad array of persons from the Iranian plateau and/or speaking the Elamite language, but many of whom may not have recognized themselves by that name. More ephemeral were the explicit invocations of tribal identity made by Zimri-Lim of Mari, Rīm-Sin of Larsa, and Ḫammurabi of Babylon, in claims to "Amorite" identity. These claims were few in number, relatively vague (e.g., "RN, father/king of the Amorite land" rather than "RN, Amorite chief" – as much as a claim of belonging to the tribe) and restricted to a few generations when tribal-state politics were deeply entangled (i.e., the late 19th / early 18th centuries).

Still, ethnonyms sometimes seem to have corresponded to real and clear ethnic differences. For instance, both tribal structures and language differences are known for Amorites, Kassites, and Aramaeans, three groups whose settlement in Babylonia had significant effects at the "national" political level at different moments. Their trajectories differed: Amorite and Aramaean groups pursued a mix of tribal separateness and urban integration in the Early/Middle

---

[39] See esp. Bahrani 2006: esp. 54–57 and De Graef 1999a–b. In most cases, there is not sufficient evidence about lineage, settlement patterns, or lifeways to define the socio-political organization of these "tribes" in anthropological terms.

[40] For an example of ethno-linguistic groups "submerged" in the textual record, see Macginnis 2012.

Bronze and Iron Age, respectively, whereas the Kassites almost completely (if gradually) assimilated to Babylonian culture in the Middle/Late Bronze Age.

At any rate, "tribal" people and ethnic "others" were a constant feature of Babylonian life. In the OB, we find them at all textual interstices: Sutaeans giving loans and holding city property; Subarians trafficked as slaves; Turukkeans serving as mercenaries; men with Hurrian names as field-hands; Elamites as the owners of fields. We see Kassites settled in "camps," Hanaeans in countryside fortresses, and unnamed groups just called "enemies." Between the questions of assimilation/integration, practices of nomenclature, and evidence for separateness, we cannot make unilateral statements about whether or how such groups were "networks of power"; but neither can they be dismissed as irrelevant to the question. As with modern tribalism, we see evidence for ethnically named persons and groups settled in cities exhibiting both socioeconomic integration as well as distinctiveness. In other instances, we read of such people settled in rural contexts, separate from cities but not necessarily from states, with their influence being primarily territorial, controlling resources or patches of land that only notionally "belonged" to states.

2.7 Immaterial Aspects of Political Power

Previously, I have discussed actors and groups who did not always directly "belong" to a state sector, but who nevertheless intersected with the organization of state power. Here, I consider three spheres of practice in which these interests often intersected or came into conflict: literary production, epistolary culture, and legal rhetoric. These arenas could be used to further state power but also to assert the authority of non-state actors and institutions. They all produced textual precipitates that were "material" (i.e., in their written form) but reflected immaterial discourses, both producing and responding to political authority. These show us some of the ways in which people *thought* about political life – their own roles, agencies, and contingencies – rather than reifying it, revealing some infrastructural powers that may not be so readily apparent.

As to literature: I have made brief reference to different types of scribes, in palaces, temples, and private households. Most tablets ever written were administrative or legal rather than literary texts, that is, the copying and composition of narratives, hymns, and "knowledge" texts such as omens, lexical lists, and historical accounts. The question raised by Moreno García is whether literary production reflected a scribal culture autonomous of political control. Indeed, the investment of scribal energy in Mesopotamian state literature was clearly great, in royal inscriptions, year-names, hymns, and epics, not to mention the tens of thousands of practical documents drafted to effect palace business. Given how much literature was openly celebratory of royal authority, we may doubt whether much of it ever reflected a critical voice expressing ideas independent or even skeptical of political authority. Scribal and political cultures were so closely intertwined that there are often only very subtle clues that critical or corrosive "voices" existed alongside authoritative ones (see Robson 2013).

One approach in finding those voices has been to identify literary themes that evoke anything less than royal perfection: The hubris of Gilgameš and Naram-Sîn, proverbs accusing palaces of venality and corruption, the *Lament for Sumer and Ur* depicting King Ibbi-Sîn "immobilized by fear," "weeping bitterly," and taken away to Elam as a prisoner in chains. There are also motifs that celebrated and prioritized non-royal forms of authority (gods, temples, scribes, or fathers). The number of examples is not endless, but enough exists to show that scribes at least had the capacity to express less-than-celebratory ideas about kings and extol other kinds of social power. We may note also that OB literary production was (as in other periods) centered in cities that had no substantial kingship traditions: Nippur, Sippar, and Ur. Exactly what is implied by the apparent geographic segregation of political and literary authority is unclear, but some distinctions pertained. It would be hard to say that any of this constitutes a sustained native critique of kings or kingship. The types of criticisms were too diverse: Some works disparaged royal impiety, some deplored greed, and others merely pointed out fallibility. It is difficult to identify any collective scribal *Tendenz* – any sharp and focused critique of power.

But it is worth considering that the scribes who copied all these works were the *same* scribes who routinely copied literature celebratory of kingship. As I have written elsewhere of this apparent paradox,

> The meeting of these literatures in scribal households shows that political diglossia was necessary to mediate between state and subject; that sanctioned forms of criticism were part of the apparatus creating subjectivity. Significantly, the royal literature and laments did not engage the sympathetic imagination of the proverbs; attempts to naturalize the state as representative polis and theological community were not accepted at face value within the bureaucratic ranks. Yet neither did the proverbs, dubious though they were of the state's probity and ability, directly challenge its authority to *act* in the capacities to which it pretended, or the premises on which it did so. To target the state's venality and ineptitude was not to say that its intrusions into households, temples, or law courts were inherently inappropriate. If this demarcates anything, it is the categorical autonomy of the Mesopotamian "state" and "civil society" (Richardson 2018: 273).

In short, autonomy and criticism are not necessarily antithetical to state power. Rather, state permission of criticism in discrete terms and modest quantities actually underscores that states allowed and even encouraged dissent so long as it stayed within certain limits.[41] In tolerating a cultural space in which criticisms could be diffused and dissipated and problems thought through, states benefitted from the same literary sphere so crucial for producing state ideology.

Epistolary culture also carved out social spaces autonomous of state power. I have earlier touched on the letter-writing of private householders and merchants, with thousands of letters covering every conceivable subject, from pigs to politics. This was a mode of communication used by a community of actors often independent of palace or temple control. The sending and receiving of letters was exercised freely, without institutional regulation. Any person literate enough to command a relatively small repertoire of cuneiform signs (perhaps eighty or so) could draft and read a letter. I have elsewhere argued (2022) that letters give evidence not only for noninstitutional concerns but for the emergence of a class-consciousness for those styling themselves as *awīlū*, "gentlemen." The question of whether the "gentlemen" belonged to state organizations is not really my focus here. The main point is that so much state business was affected *through* a literary form often used outside the palace walls. The OB is when we first see palaces extensively relying on letters as their most important mode of communication. The best example is the enormous corpus of letters from Mari, reflecting a kingdom carrying out its most urgent business by letter – warfare, trade, intelligence, and statecraft.[42]

More than their specific and diverse contents, we should consider the differences implied between states that relied on letter-writing and those (mostly earlier ones) that did not. Non-letter writing states relied to a greater degree on direct command and less on explanation and persuasion. They were characterized by distances small enough to allow simple commands to be relayed face-to-face; did not require the distributed apparatus of chancelleries to archive received letters and compose replies; were less shaped, sociologically speaking, by an officialdom schooled in the politesse of formal communication. The impact of the letter genre on OB states, therefore, cannot be overstated. The practice of letter-writing generated a distinct discursive authority through writers' claims about knowledge and communicative reach. Of course, the "niceties" in these letters were mostly phatic: Substantially, letters were mostly complaints about things left undone or not done right, not notes of congratulation reporting

---

[41] Cf. Islamic concepts of *mubah* and *makruh*, that which is "permitted" or "disapproved of" but not "forbidden" (*haram*); and the mid-1950s "Hundred Flowers Movement" during which time the Chinese Communist Party (briefly) encouraged criticism of the Party.

[42] I am keenly aware that we still do not have the archives of other OB palaces of Babylon, Larsa, Ešnunna, etc. Cf. smaller palace archives published by Eidem 2010 (Tell Leilan/Šehna) and Abed 2018 ("Basi City").

that everything was fine. For this reason, letter-writing states give us better information about mistakes and problems than non-letter-writing states, which primarily churned out reports about normative activities.

Finally, I must mention the intense flurry of legal activity that characterized the OB. The half-dozen law collections of the period epitomize the extension of the law into many areas – not only regulating civil and criminal affairs, but conflicts in commercial and even family life. Crucially, the laws studiously avoided pronouncing on ethical, religious, or moral questions, matters outside state purview. But the law codes were just the tip of the iceberg: OB texts reflect legal process in lawsuits, depositions, contracts (and model contracts), oaths, royal regulations, and scholarly lists of legal phraseology; for legal actors such as judges, bailiffs, witnesses, plaintiffs, defendants, assemblies, scribes-of-record, elders, and city authorities; venues such as city gates, riverbanks, and temples; material apparatus such as seals, boundary pegs, judge's chairs (giš.gu.za *dayānūtu*), and divine emblems. Every humdrum contract, the text type most emblematic of the age, was of course a legal document; though these were not necessarily executed by legal officials per se, the act and fact of their witnessing and sealing made even the smallest barley loan a legally enforceable transaction. It cannot be emphasized how much this differs from previous periods: These features may have existed individually in prior times, but only in the OB do we see the frequency and range of legal forms and rhetoric being focused on such a wide range of activities.

What was the relationship of law to state power? We might deduce from Hammurabi's long and impressive collection of just decisions that the Babylonian state routinely pronounced law and exercised its application – that legal order was an important component of state power. But what I see is that OB states rarely exercised their judicial authority (indeed, we can sometimes see them actively *avoiding* it); most legal processes were conducted by local officials according to local custom. As I have argued, the credit that OB states took for assimilating law to royal power was a triumph of political rhetoric rather than instrumental control. States mimicked and appropriated legal rhetoric mostly to claim credit for the entirety of "justice" rather than to appoint judges, mete out punishment, run law courts by "code," or administer law *as a function of government*. Nor was local justice universally popular. Plenty of letters about lawsuits complain about wrong decisions and the unfairness of venues; at least one proverb inveighs against judges "who despise justice, cursing with the right hand," "abominations to Šamaš," the god of justice.

None of this should persuade us that law was unimportant or somehow "false." To the contrary, the emulation of legal power by states shows us just how attractive it was, and how potent its discursive power was in the culture, regulating so many aspects of civil and commercial life. This situation was largely an outcome of the interaction sphere of the epistolary community of "gentlemen" – it did not originate within the state sector. But if law was not a state power, imitation certainly was: States were excellent chameleons, imitating powers found in other areas of cultural life and claiming them as natural and appropriate for kings. The long-term result was that later ages accepted royal claims about justice uncritically. Scribes in later centuries time routinely copied out Hammurabi's stele, and may have misunderstood his "collection of just decisions" as a set of accepted rules – a "law code." This may have been a basis for accepting that it was normal for states to exercise justice exclusively and preemptively. On this hypothesis, it would therefore be unsurprising that no Babylonian king after Hammurabi for a thousand years ever bothered to write out a "law code" again:[43] the premise of legal authority had been baked in through invented tradition.

2.8 State Power: Limits and Potentials

I see ancient states as existing in a balance of "low power" with the social sectors over which they proposed to exercise authority, including temple institutions, cities, kinship groups, mercantile networks, tribes, transhumant bands, and rural populations – even the Crown's own body of officials (see further Richardson 2012). Although these groups never had the power to challenge state predominance outright, they always had enough to complicate it. From this "low power" reading, three points may be made about state power. First, we should not assess royal literature in terms of fact and fiction – that states either did or didn't do particular things – but as *claims*, a "wish list" for the powers they aspired to have. A careful reading of state claims as presumptive, rather than "true" or "false," can help us write a history of not only how states "actually worked," but also how they worked to bring their powers and authorities into being. Second, beyond purporting to describe functional powers (to enforce law, regulate commerce, provide security, etc.), royal literature discursively coded those powers as normal and appropriate to states *rather than to other groups and institutions*. These roles had to be presented as more than just desirable acts, but as moral goods natural to states and not to other actors. States thus had to build governmentality as much as government. Third, time was on the side of states in these projects: even if powers were not fully operative when first claimed, later ages came to see the inscriptions claiming them as descriptions of real accomplishments. Processes

---

[43] It is not clear that the so-called "Neo-Babylonian Laws" were attributed to a ruler (Roth 1995: 144).

of political collapse, social forgetting, and the reconstitution of new states allowed successive epochs to look back on previous ages and read old claims as historical facts. Babylonians in 1750 BC most likely understood Hammurabi's stele of judgments as exemplary decisions rather than as strictly enforceable laws – knowing that actual cases were judged according to varying local standards by judges, elders, or assemblies, rather than by the king himself. But Babylonians in later centuries, when portions of the "codex" were copied and recopied, may have seen the text as a factual account of how law was traditionally exercised, with royal legal authority clearly preeminent or exclusive. In such ways, states encouraged and invited the "parts" to work with "wholes" which had not yet cohered.

At any given point in Mesopotamian history, we can identify gaps and lapses in royal power. But we need not to consider these limitations as evidence of state insufficiency. We might just as well reflect on how shortcomings in ancient state power compare with modern-day states which must sometimes compete with warlords, drug cartels, hacker collectives, and other substate actors who may mimic state power in some respects even as they contest it. Meanwhile, *supra*-state forces such as global capitalism, international media, and cosmopolitan culture erode the local powers of individual states. None of this must lead us to conclude that modern states therefore do not "work" and should be entirely thrown away. It only means that states are not eternal, transhistorical, or exclusive forms of social organization, but historically particular and contingent forms – ones which must always work *with and against* other kinds of actors, never quite done with their project.

The "low power" model invites us to consider that political claims can be *productive* of future state authority prospectively even when they do not reflect present realities. In this view, it matters less whether Hammurabi's "laws" were used as advertised; it mattered more that these ideas were on their way to lever people to participate in the state project. We should not discount the imaginative power that the audiences for political claims brought to reading them, including the role that the lower ranks of elites played in broadcasting political messages and symbols verbally and performatively to nonliterate subjects (Liverani 2014). The systematic propagation of ideas itself produced *subjectivity* by naming the terms of participation, even when subjects were all too aware of the shortcomings of state claims in terms of reality. Applying a reader-reception theory need not be much more complicated than understanding that citizens could temper their doubts about state claims with aspirations that they might become true. This was a triumph of hope over experience, repeated century after century, the engine that incentivized the participation of elites, sub-elites, and informal leaders in state projects.

So, did the parts of Babylonian states work together as a whole? Were Mesopotamian central states substantially operative of the local networks notionally subordinate to them? I would say "yes" *if* we understand state power to be something other than a monopolist control over law, membership, territory, taxation, and (of course) legitimate violence as we understand it today. "Yes" *if* we understand state power to primarily be the creation and maintenance of infrastructural and institutional mechanisms to contain and channel competition, dissent, and personal ambition. The purpose of this power was only secondarily to run state business with maximum efficiency. Its primary purpose was to delimit the arenas within which institutions and actors would interact, to provide the references and boundaries of social, economic, and political activity; in effect, to define reality more than to run the world for profit or to accomplish specific ends. In this view, it would hardly matter how completely states "controlled" their officers, delegates, and resources in hard and precise terms. The paramount achievement was to keep control over the discursive basis of power negotiation. Every day in which cooperation and conflict were defined by state language and forms was a victory for state power – the organization of what was possible.

3 Power Organization in Egypt

3.1 Introduction

Ancient Egypt is frequently regarded as the first territorial state in history and one of the earliest and most complete examples of a centralized and bureaucratic monarchy (Figure 7). Not by chance, its rich iconographic and textual legacy has contributed to such a view. Temple scenes and rock reliefs in border areas represent the king as the center of the world, crushing Egypt's enemies, receiving tribute, overseeing officials and members of the court and enjoying the protection of the gods, a message that strengthens the centrality of kings and officials as heads of a hierarchically organized society. Other texts, such as official records and laudatory compositions, celebrate the king's majesty, his unrestricted power and his privileged position as mediator between humans and gods, his will being the supreme source of authority and decision-making, implemented through a myriad of scribes, officials and royal agents. Finally, administrative papyri creates the impression of a meticulous and all-encompassing bureaucracy that efficiently controlled the population and activities of the country (Grajetzki 2006; Oppenheim et al. 2015).

However, a critical analysis of these sources and their ideological claims provides a more balanced perspective, particularly in the light of administrative documents and archaeological evidence. As I see it, the turn of the second

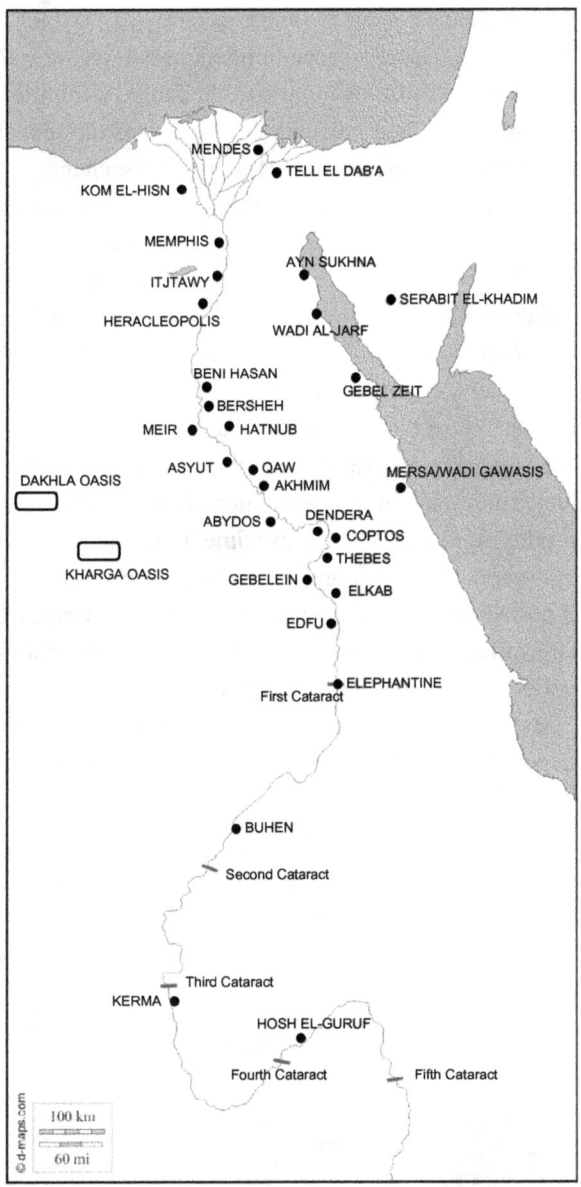

Figure 7 Map of ancient Egypt (©Juan Carlos Moreno García).

millennium BC (2100–1800 BC) offers a unique glimpse into the actual organization of power in ancient Egypt, a view that departs in many aspects from the ideal representations of authority elaborated by kings and scribes, allegedly rooted in old traditions. These centuries constituted a turning point that contrasts sharply with the preceding and following periods, when royal power and governmental organization seemed more centralized, stable, and durable. Therefore, I understand the early second millennium BC as a transitional period in which kings struggled to overcome the challenges – political, economic, social, and cultural – that had precipitated the end of the monarchy and the fragmentation of the country around 2160 BC. This change came after an exceptionally long period of political unity and apparent solid monarchical rule between 3100 and 2160 BC. However, during the relatively short-lived period of reunification that followed (2050–1800 BC), kings faced considerable challenges, and their authority appeared somewhat precarious, built on fragile conditions, sometimes contested by internal and external powers and, in the end, prone to political fragmentation again (Figure 8) (Moreno García 2021).

This means that the restoration of the old monarchic order and traditions around 2050 BC was more a wishful claim than a real achievement (Figure 9). This circumstance may explain the importance of cultural innovations aiming to stress the centrality of kings. At the same time, those same innovations reveal a certain anxiety about the very foundations and possibilities of royal action. In this way, this period opened the possibility of detecting crucial factors rarely referred to in the official record but that determined the possibilities for building a durable royal order in Egypt. These factors shaped the pharaonic balance of power, its crystallization and reconstruction over time, a dynamic process marked by negotiation, alliances and variable forms of wealth distribution

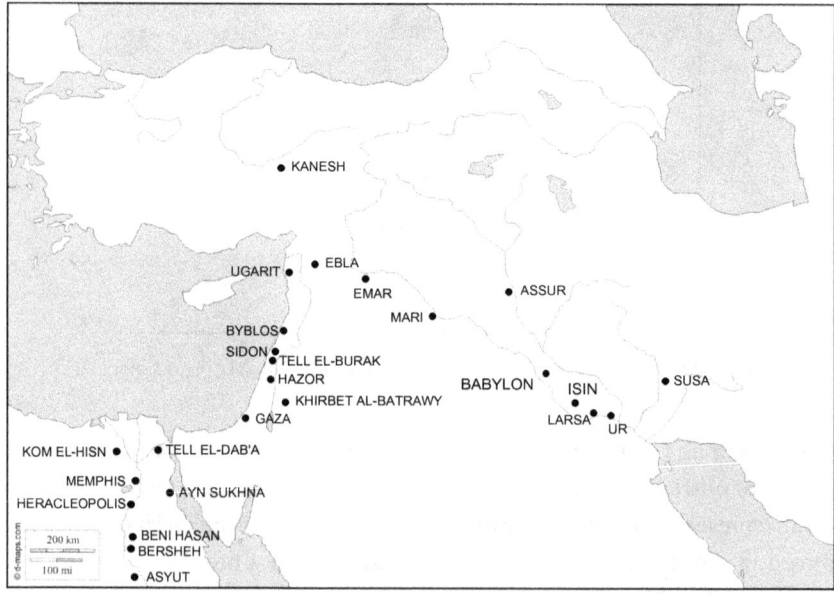

Figure 8 Map of the ancient Near East (©Juan Carlos Moreno García).

Figure 9 Relief of Mentuhotep II, the king who reunified Egypt around 2040 BC. Metropolitan Museum of Art, CC0, via Wikimedia Commons. https://commons.wikimedia.org/wiki/File:Relief_of_Nebhepetre_Mentuhotep_II_and_the_Goddess_Hathor_MET_DP322047.jpg

between the kings, elites and sub-elites of the country. In the end, the pharaohs' power depended on the successful integration of diverse sources of authority into the structures of the monarchy – some of them potentially alternative to the ruling kings. This meant testing the capacity of kings to co-opt leaders, keeping an equilibrium between different factions of the elite, producing cultural and ceremonial sources of legitimacy and, finally, tying the interests of the elites to those of the monarchy. In the end, the decisions that the pharaohs took between 2050–1800 BC to assert their authority provide us with a unique opportunity to analyze the foundations, limits and interplay of the diverse sources of power operating in Egypt behind a rhetoric that stressed centralization, continuity and tradition (Quirke 1991a; Grajetzki 2009; Moreno García 2017).

I will use two examples to illustrate these points. Khnumhotep II, a provincial leader of Beni Hasan in Middle Egypt, mentioned in his biography that the kings had appointed him and his father as "mayors" of this locality. Since such nominations fell on the same family, it seems that kings limited themselves to formally confer power and its transmission within the single local ruling families. Incidentally, Khnumhotep II's grandfather (Khnumhotep I) boasted about helping pharaoh Amenemhet I (1985–1956 BC) to consolidate royal rule over Middle Egypt by expelling an unidentified enemy of the crown.

A similar situation emerged at Elkab three centuries later. The *Stèle Juridique* of Karnak describes a procedure aiming to ensure that the succession to the governorship of Elkab remained in the hands of one dominant local family. Elkab was then a firm support to the regional kingdom of Thebes, and its ruling family was part of the dominant elite in southern Egypt, related by marriage to the Theban kings. According to this document, the rightful heir to the position of "mayor" was heavily indebted to another member of this family. When the payment of this debt was demanded, his only recourse was to offer succession to the governorship to his relative in satisfaction (Eyre 2013: 149–153). Both examples reveal that, beyond rhetorical claims about absolute power, kings had to cope with powerful provincial families deeply rooted in the territories they controlled for generations, and relied on their fidelity if royal authority was to be accepted outside the capital. However, the crucial support these groups provided to the monarchy could also turn into overt hostility, even rebellion, and provoke the collapse of royal authority, as had happened around 2160 BC.

These examples attract my attention because they concern the highest provincial elite. However, the interests of these elites were not limited to the territories they ruled. Their strategies aimed to get access to the court, hold high positions in the royal administration and join the influential core of courtiers who surrounded the kings as well. Marriages with other prominent families (including royals), integration into patronage networks headed by high officials and influential courtiers, and participation in rituals centered on pharaohs and dynastic gods helped achieve such strategies. At the same time, elites pursued tight control over their local bases of power. Temples were fundamental in this respect. As providers of legitimation, income (fields, offerings, prebends, and remunerated priesthoods), status, and coveted contacts with the royal sphere – since kings donated land and precious equipment to provincial sanctuaries –, local nobles usually monopolized the control of provincial temples and the most relevant ritual positions (Moreno García 2006; Willems 2014: 4–58). What is more, the tombs and chapels of noble ancestors sometimes became cult centers in which prominent local people placed their statues and votive monuments to show their allegiance to dominant local families. The cases of the chapel of Heqaib at Elephantine and Isi at Edfu are excellent examples of this practice (Franke 1994; Farout 2009). As for lesser cult offices in local sanctuaries, they were usually left in the hands of clients and people of inferior status. Hence, priestly offices were avidly sought after, even bought and sold.

Some sources of local power remain poorly documented for the period considered. An example concerns agricultural and production centers founded by the crown in the provinces: agricultural estates, royal stalls, work camps, harbors, mines, quarries, and even customs facilities. Their management in the name of the king opened further possibilities to accumulate wealth and prestige in the local sphere. Finally, officials and nobles, both courtly and provincial, were honored in public ceremonies at the palace and received substantial income and gifts when they accomplished specific missions or performed their ordinary duties in the royal administration efficiently. Being part of royal or princely retinues was another occasion to get income derived from the "houses" or estates of nobles and the royal family. The *Tale of Sinuhe* describes this practice: Upon his return from a long exile in the Levant, Sinuhe was accepted in the royal court. He was then given a house and a garden that had previously belonged to a courtier and was rebuilt, while the royal palace delivered meals to him "three times, four times a day apart from what the royal children gave without a moment's pause." Finally, a tomb was built for him in a prestigious necropolis, specialized craftsmen decorated it, and he received mortuary priests as well as a funerary estate that included a garden, "as is done for a Companion of the first rank." The finishing touch was his statue overlaid with gold and electrum that the king ordered to be made for Sinuhe (Parkinson 1997: 42–43).

Temples and the royal palace appear thus as essential nodes in an "elite sociability" that helped hold together the small upper class that ruled the country and, to a lesser extent, the sub-elites that held power in the countryside. A shared official culture (both written and visual), as well as common values, codes and beliefs expressed through a rich body of literary compositions and inscriptions, celebrated hierarchy, loyalty and elevated moral principles that, supposedly, should guide the behavior of officials and authorities alike (Vernus 2010). This, obviously, only represents the "official" view about good power and the ideal exercise of authority from a top-down perspective. I see an alternative perspective, one putting house(hold)s and kin interests at the very center of the power strategies power that the elites followed instead. Not by chance, this was a period in which personal inscriptions and ritual compositions described the composition of such households in detail. Centered on a *pater familias* and a prestige residence, they included substantial private assets such as fields, gardens and cattle, but also a myriad of people, from relatives to servants and many other categories of people, designated by terms like "friends," "companions," "citizens" or "colleagues." High-status people controlled extensive social networks that helped strengthen their influence, wealth and local support and enhance their prestige and authority. These informal networks bound together the highest elite and influential people from a more modest social background whose importance at the local level cannot be underestimated. Usually designated by generic terms like "great ones" or "chiefs," they provided a crucial link between the upper society and the ordinary people, between the palatial sphere and the rural world. Little is known about them, but, judging from scattered references as well as from sources from other periods, it was a social sector integrated by village chiefs, wealthy peasants, local dignitaries, temple staff, and property managers employed by the elite and important institutions. It seems that merchants, scribes, low-rank officials, "businesspeople" (including women), and, quite probably, rich people living in cities were also part of this world. When conflicts erupted and formal chains of command failed, such actors – and the informal networks of power they controlled – became more visible in the sources. It was then that seeking support from powerful protectors, the use of bribes, and the sale of property – even of oneself – to influential patrons in exchange for help were indispensable to get justice (or escape from it), avoid abuse or get access to coveted positions and lucrative business (Moreno García 2013, 2019: 61–108).

3.2 The Role of the Provinces

No do I see the contrast between the ideal and the actual organization of power more strongly than in the provinces and their integration into the kingdom's administrative structure. A historiographical tradition going back to the late 19th century AD has interpreted the provinces as the primary administrative units in the country's territorial organization, together with cities and their districts.

The premises for this view are threefold. On the one hand, it was assumed retrospectively that the territorial administration of the Hellenistic period (332–30 BC), based on *nomarchs* or provincial governors, was an inheritance from previous periods of Egyptian history. On the other hand, it was accepted that the canonic lists of provinces inscribed in many monuments – like the White Chapel of Senwosret I – corresponded to an actual administrative structure, irrespective of the ideological and ritual considerations underlying their representation in those monuments. Finally, it derived from the intellectual background of many Egyptologists who believed that pharaonic Egypt was the first territorial state in history and that its longevity was based on an efficient authority and a well-organized administration. Accordingly, ancient Egypt should reproduce features characteristic of *modern* states and become a prestigious precedent of the modern centralized states that emerged in the 19th century AD, particularly in France and Germany. Not by chance did Gaston Maspero (1846–1916) in France and Eduard Meyer (1855–1930) in Germany become the foremost advocates of this interpretation. Both of them wrote at the turn of the 19th century, when France and Germany struggled to build solid central powers after the French defeat in the Franco-Prussian war (1870–1871) and the unification of several German states into a single monarchy, the Second Reich (1871–1918). According to their views, modern states shared features such as a rational organization of power, exclusive sovereignty over a territory with clear borders, a strong hierarchical bureaucracy at the direct service of the ruler(s), administrative departments with clearly defined functions and competences, a developed tax system, a monopoly in the exercise of justice and legitimate force (police, armed forces), and a fluid circulation of instructions and information from rulers and officials to subjects. Therefore, Maspero, Mayer, and many other historians thought that "advanced" ancient states also reproduced these features and were the remote prestigious precedents of the modern nation-states (Moreno García 2019).

In this perspective, Egyptian titles were equated with modern bureaucratic positions and their holders to contemporary civil servants. Hence, a "great chief of a province" was interpreted as a "provincial governor" or *nomarch*. However, "great chiefs of a province" are only documented in a few provinces, mostly in Middle Egypt, so other titles were assimilated to the category of *nomarch* too to justify that a homogeneous administration covered all of Egypt. This was the case of "mayors" (*haty-a*) of a city or a province. Another problem is that the duties of those "great chiefs of a province" are never clearly stated or defined in any source of the period considered. Perhaps more problematic, they are systematically absent in the sources that describe in detail the kingdom's administrative structure (*onomastica*, compositions such as the *Duties of the*

Vizier, royal decrees). Finally, the distribution of rank and function titles differed significantly from province to province. To sum up, the idea of a homogeneous and hierarchical administrative organization implemented throughout Egypt seems an anachronistic projection into the past (Ilin-Tomich 2017; Moreno García 2019: 61–108).

On the contrary, cities and nobles constituted the backbone of the power structure for the countryside. Genealogical evidence reveals that it was usual that a powerful family controlled the main institutions (temple, royal estates, main city) of the province where its members lived and were buried, at least for eight generations in the best-documented cases. Their role and status were recognized by the king, who bestowed them the honorific title of "great chief of a province." It first appeared in the second half of the third millennium BC. However, if the title was then used in many provinces of Upper Egypt – not a single case is documented in Lower Egypt – its utilization became much more restricted in the early centuries of the second millennium BC. Not only was it practically absent in Lower Egypt, but its attestations in Middle Egypt were restricted to a few provinces, practically limited to the area between Qaw and Beni Hasan, separated by 150 kms. A distinctive feature of these provinces is that their nobles displayed an astonishing capacity to accumulate wealth and political influence, judging by their impressive tombs and the high positions they held. Almost royal in scale and exquisitely decorated, these tombs give some clues about the actual balance of power prevailing in Egypt after the reunification (ca. 2050 BC). Furthermore, these provinces were located at strategic crossroads of fluvial and land routes, and their leaders were involved in exchanges with foreign areas and, in some cases, monitored the arrival of foreign goods into Egypt. Wealth derived from international trade – textiles, minerals, aromatic plants, precious metals, exotic goods – which apparently played an important role in their political status. Therefore, it is not by chance that these noble families, who had supported the northern Heracleopolitan kingdom during the previous period of political division of Egypt, shifted their loyalty to the Theban kings and made thus possible the restoration of a unified monarchy around 2050 BC. Their support nevertheless came at a price, as if the new pharaohs were forced to recognize and respect the interests of these nobles, who accumulated power and political influence unmatched by any other provincial leader of their time (Moreno García 2017). Hence, an unbalanced territorial distribution of power prevailed, when some provinces accumulated wealth, influence and resources while their leaders kept considerable interests both in foreign exchange and in the kingdom's affairs as, for instance, viziers and holders of relevant palatial positions. For example, nobles from Qaw and Bersheh provided the majority of mayors who ruled the funerary complex built by pharaoh Senwosret III at Abydos (Wegner 2010).

In my opinion, this unbalanced organization produced two main consequences. On the one hand, the leaders of the most important provinces exerted a profound influence on the affairs of the state. Yet they also linked their destiny to the monarchy, as this institution remained a crucial tool to preserve their privileged position and interests, particularly in foreign matters. Thus, any monarchical crisis had the disturbing potential to harm them and expose their vulnerability because of their dependence on the state's resources and the role of kings as mediators between elite factions. On the other hand, provincial elites remained a fragmented and diversified social group, with a core of great influential nobles in Middle Egypt followed at a considerable distance by nobles of lesser status – perhaps Elephantine and Khalwa being the only exceptions, at least for some periods. Therefore, a fragmented provincial nobility with no shared political goals could hardly project their influence collectively into the state. This circumstance allowed kings to limit and manipulate the ambitions of the local elites. Furthermore, any failure to preserve their position and fortune opened fresh opportunities to ambitious nobles of lesser status, eager to improve their condition (Moreno García 2019: 61– 6).

3.3 The Elusive World of Cities

Cities remain one of the most elusive aspects of the social, political and economic life of pharaonic Egypt. According to many authors, cities are one of the most conspicuous features of early civilized life and sophisticated sociopolitical organization. However, Egyptian urbanism still remains insufficiently known for the period considered. Only the recent work of Nadine Moeller and other archaeologists is providing new evidence about the urban layout and the role of cities in the very late third millennium and the early centuries of the second millennium BC (Moeller 2016, 2023). What emerges from their work is a distinctive pattern of urbanism, different from that of Mesopotamia or Syria during the same period. Egyptian cities were tiny settlements (about 15 ha in the case of Edfu, perhaps only four in Dendera), but archaeology reveals that they flourished when the monarchy collapsed after 2160 BC and afterward. Residential neighborhoods expanded then at Elephantine, Edfu, Dendera and Abydos. A category of moderately affluent people inhabited these communities, and the capacity of some facilities excavated (silos, manufacturing areas) exceeded the needs of a nuclear family or mere subsistence. The use of seals expanded too, and points to the increasing importance of sealing in everyday transactions and the mobilization of commodities in the domestic sphere, perhaps for sale or distribution to subordinates, clients and markets. The written record from this period confirms this impression. Seals and sealed documents are frequently mentioned in sales of fields, houses, and even priestly services. At the same time, many sources emphasize the importance of wealthy households as centers of extensive patronage networks that included urban dwellers (*demiu, niutiu*). As I have shown, stelae, decorated coffins and prestigious goods owned by people bearing no official titles confirm the existence of an affluent sector of people involved in private economic activities (Moreno García 2024).

Four consequences may be inferred from this evidence. Firstly, organic urban development was a slow process in Egypt, quite different from the importance and scale visible in Mesopotamia and Syria at the same time, not to speak about earlier periods (fourth and third millennium BC). Secondly, this process was concomitant with the abandonment of the old network of agricultural and storage centers of the crown (called *hwt*) founded in the third millennium BC, spread across all Egypt and that had been the primary nodes of settlement organization and the backbone of the royal tax system until 2160 BC. This may explain why cities and city gods became crucial in creating social identities from 2100 BC onward. Furthermore, urban growth was concomitant with the expansion of riverine trade (*demi* "city, town" designated the harbor area of a city initially, while *meryt* "quay" also meant market), as if the previous state-controlled system of circulation of goods along the Nile, based on royal estates like the *hwt*, had been replaced by a nonroyal and city-centered one. Finally, cities remained small, so the potential strength of organized city bodies capable of making their demands heard and their interests respected or enhanced by rulers (from kings to local nobles) seems negligible at best. A clear trace of traders' neighborhoods has yet to be identified, in contrast with Mesopotamian cities like Ur or Larsa. Moreover, there is no reference to collective bodies of "citizens" in charge of local government and administration (Moreno García 2019: 88–96).

Occasional mentions to "councils of the district" reveal that this institution assumed local administrative measures and acted as a mediator with the central administration. Nevertheless, the sources remain elusive about its composition. Some officials held the title of "member of the district council," so it may be possible that these councils gathered a combination of officials, royal agents and local notables who deliberated about matters concerning taxation, justice and services due to the crown. In fact, only men of a certain status were qualified enough to become members of local councils: "if you have the rank of a gentleman (lit. son of a man) who belongs to a council (*qnbt*) ... " (Parkinson 1997: 259). A juridical expression present in wills and other transactions from this period refers to the possessions of nobles and officials "in the city and the countryside." Consequently, both social groups were potentially influential actors in city affairs because of their economic interests there. It was typical that provincial nobles raised and led local militia formed by citizens who, otherwise, seemed to have no voice in the management of the localities where they lived. Only a fascinating fragmentary passage of *The Teaching for (king) Merykare*, a literary composition describing events set in the early 21st century BC, refers to citizens susceptible to falling under the influence of demagogues and trouble-makers who challenged the king's authority (Parkinson 1997: 217–218). As the end of the third millennium BC was a period when the good opinion and legitimacy provided by cities became highly regarded by local nobles and officials, I think it is possible that any potential political influence of "citizens" declined rapidly afterward, once the country was reunified and the monarchy restored around 2050 BC (Moreno García 2024).

This is also evident in the case of expressions formed by *nedjes*. This term ("small, modest") was used around 2160–2050 BC with a new sense, that of independent individuals whose wealth derived from their effort, not from any reward or service to the kings (Figure 10). The sudden popularity of this term – even officials and nobles described themselves as *nedjes* in their inscriptions – points to a potential new political force in this period, when the monarchy had collapsed and power was disputed by competing regional powers. Texts from this period refer to the population of particular localities and regions as encompassing "great ones" (*aa*) and *nedjes*. Inscriptions from Asyut and Hatnub routinely refer to the protection that their leaders dispensed to the *nedjes* in these troubled times. Once the monarchy was restored, the term *nedjes* figured mainly in literary compositions, whereas its use declined sharply in the inscriptions and epithets employed by the officials of the new administration, who never identified themselves as *nedjes*. Therefore, it is tempting to see in this term a marker of the social changes that occurred between 2160 and 2000 BC when local audiences and city residents became a force to be considered, at least formally, after the monarchy had collapsed. Afterward, their influence and status declined when the monarchy and its oligarchic organization of power prevailed in Egypt again around 2050 BC. It was then that genealogies and lineage pride figured prominently in the monuments of provincial leaders and "mayors" instead, making it possible to follow the whereabouts of some powerful families for generations (Moreno García 1997: 32–45).

3.4 Cities and Territorial Articulation

Judging from the archaeological evidence, cities remained relatively modest settlements in the first half of the second millennium BC, both in size and

Figure 10 Stela of a dignitary of the First Intermediate Period. ArchaiOptix, CC BY-SA 4.0 <https://creativecommons.org/licenses/by-sa/4.0>, via Wikimedia Commons. https://commons.wikimedia.org/wiki/File: Relief_stele_of_Rehu_from_the_first_intermediate_period_01.jpg

political capacity – capital cities like Thebes, Avaris/Tell el-Dabʿa and (probably) Memphis being the main exceptions. The best-documented examples reveal that the smaller cities covered only a few hectares and hardly matched their contemporary counterparts in Mesopotamia or Syria and their burgeoning trading neighborhoods and craft areas. This probably explains why Egyptian cities never became significant nodes of political and economic initiative despite the more favorable conditions prevalent in the early second millennium BC, when cities and "citizens" figure prominently in private inscriptions as sources of legitimacy for ambitious leaders. Furthermore, the apparent oligarchical monarchy which was restored around 2050 BC, based on an alliance between powerful provincial nobles and the royal court, did little to enhance the political stature of cities. Harbor areas increased their importance along the Nile and replaced the old network of agricultural and storage centers of the crown scattered across the country. At the same time, the monarchy retained a substantial influence in shaping the settlement organization of the country, at least in critical strategic areas. Finally, trade routes and communities of herders settled in the Nile Valley also left their mark on Egyptian soil.

The reunification of Egypt did not imply a mere return to the settlement organization that existed before 2160 BC. The last two centuries of the third millennium BC witnessed the abandonment of many localities situated on the eastern branch of the Nile in Lower Egypt, from about thirty to merely six (Małecka-Drozd 2021). In contrast, several settlements flourished then along the western axis of the Nile in the Delta, like Kom el-Hisn, Barnugi and others, a circumstance probably linked to increased contact between Egypt and the Aegean (Moreno García 2017). However, these localities declined once the monarchy was restored around 2050 BC. Both phenomena resulted from profound changes in the commercial and mining networks of the very late third millennium BC. Copper from Feinan, Timna and Sinai was extracted and exported directly to Egypt by mobile desert populations. Hence, the role of former Egyptian mediators became superfluous, and settlements in the Eastern Delta declined or were abandoned. Not by chance, a particular category of people called *sekhetiu* (lit. countrymen) figure prominently in the administrative and literary sources of the early second millennium BC. They are autonomous people primarily attested in the easternmost Delta and surrounding desert areas and provided logistic support to the mining expeditions sent by the pharaohs to the Sinai and the northern Red Sea. Officials were explicitly appointed to deal with them. The equal importance of "marginal populations" and reduced sedentary life is visible in other regions of Egypt too. In the case of Deir el-Gebrawy, in Middle Egypt, the inscription of Henqu, a provincial leader who lived there around 2200 BC, describes that the local population had returned to more mobile lifestyles. Fishing and extensive cattle breeding were concomitant with the absence of towns, so Henqu boasted about having settled these wandering populations in towns again. However, no single elite tomb or provincial leader is attested at Deir el-Gebrawy after 2000 BC, as if this province had lost its former political status definitively and became loosely populated again (Moreno García 2017).

Sources from other areas (Fayyum, Thinis, Dendera) suggest to me that similar conditions pertained there too, as fowlers, fishermen, and herders moved across these regions, and officials were appointed to control their movements. Mobile lifestyles and more intense interactions between mobile peoples and sedentary populations characterize the end of the third millennium BC and the first centuries of the second millennium BC. It seems that such interaction was related to the increasing importance of extensive cattle breeding and, perhaps, the seasonal or permanent use of the services provided by mobile herders (cf. the peculiar representation of some herders in this period: Diego

Espinel 2019). In the case of Dendera, inscriptions from the early 21st century BC reveal that the old network of crown centers had disappeared, so the Theban king appointed officials to rule this locality and promote economic activities such as cattle breeding. As for neighboring Coptos, some people had abandoned their towns and returned to mobile lifestyles after the collapse of the monarchy around 2160 BC: "the overseer of priests Djefi sent me to (the locality of) Island-of-shenshen. I found it ruined, and I refounded it. I brought back its cattle, and I made an account of absolutely everything" (Moreno García 2020). The first attestations of new terms in the very late third millennium BC reveal the importance of extensive cattle breeding and the changes this practice introduced in the settlement organization of some regions. One of these terms is *menmenet* "cattle on the move," another one *whyt* "tribe, village." *Whyt*-villages and *menmenet*-cattle appeared first in the inscriptions of Middle Egypt, a region rich in pasture land. The iconography of its elite tombs depicts Levantine peoples and caravans of Asians and "Libyans" arriving there with their flocks and loads of minerals. In other cases, local nobles increased the economic resources of their provinces by promoting extensive cattle breeding. Hence, Imeny of Beni Hasan claimed that he had appointed managers to the cattle ranches of the province and provisioned them with 3000 bulls to deliver cattle quotas, so "I was praised for it in the Royal Domain in every year of the cattle tax." The proliferation of "clanic" *whyt*-villages in Middle Egypt suggests that mobile populations (not exclusively made up of foreigners) and their particular social structure, based on kin groups, left their mark on the local settlements and landscape of this region. This may explain the presence in Upper and Middle Egypt of many small cemeteries of itinerant Nubian populations, the Pan-Grave culture, in the first half of the second millennium BC. Further to the north, in the Fayyum, occasional references to Asians living there in Levantine settlements called *wenet* (and, in later times, in similar ones called *seger*) confirm that non-Egyptian peoples lived in these regions and introduced a settlement structure characteristic of their social organization (Moreno García 2017, 2020).

As for organic towns and cities, two distinctive features define the early second millennium BC. On the one hand, the importance of harbor facilities, to the point that the harbor area (*demi*) of towns became the synonym of "town, city." On the other hand, organic cities formed administrative units together with their districts or (called *w* in Egyptian). The old network of crown centers (*hwt*) was never restored. Only sparse references in administrative documents reveal that some still survived and provided foodstuff to the funerary complexes of the kings at Ilahun in the Fayyum region. Unfortunately, it is impossible to verify if the political and economic importance of some localities in Middle Egypt (Hermopolis, Beni Hasan, Asyut, Meir) was supported by thriving urbanism. In the case of the city of Hermopolis (close to the necropolis of Bersheh), it was initially founded on an island in the Nile. However, the river's subsequent shift to the east gradually separated its harbor area from the urban space (Toonen et al. 2022). Hence, a local inscription describes the transport of a colossal statue from the quarries of Hatnub to Hermopolis, to the harbor (*demi*) of the town (*nut*).

Compare these localities with Elephantine in southernmost Egypt. A commercial and harbor city, settled by Egyptians and Nubians whose activities were oriented toward Nubia since early times, Elephantine expanded at the turn of the third millennium BC. However, it never reached a significant size and remained a small settlement (a mere 5 ha). So the commercial and administrative relevance of Elephantine, not to speak of its role as the seat of a powerful dynasty of provincial leaders well connected with the court, hardly matched its modest size. Things were probably different in Tell el-Dab'a. The city grew from a *hwt* center of the crown, then transformed into the operational basis of the Egyptian land and sea trading expeditions to the Levant in the early second millennium BC. Later on, in the 17th and 16th centuries BC, it became one of the most important hubs of exchange of the Eastern Mediterranean and the capital of an independent kingdom in Lower Egypt. A feature shared with Elephantine was the local presence of a considerable community of foreigners, mostly Levantine and, to a lesser extent, Nubians. It has been estimated that in the 18th century BC, the site covered about 70 ha and included a substantial orthogonal area whose planned layout suggests the intervention of the crown, as opposed to Elephantine (Bietak 2018; Forstner-Müller 2021).

In other cases, the monarchy played an active role in the creation of settlements, often related to temples and royal funerary complexes. Ilahun, Abydos, some areas of Tell el-Dab'a and Qasr el-Sagha are good illustrations of such specialized localities; the latter is interpreted as a possible work camp. Work camps (*kheneret*) gained considerable importance in the territorial organization of the kingdom from 1800 BC on, at least judging from the number of officials in their charge and the papyrological and epigraphic evidence that describes their activities (Quirke 1988). There is also evidence of a substantial investment of crown resources in the creation and maintenance of infrastructure such as mining facilities (Serabit el-Khadim, Wadi el-Hudi), harbors (Ayn Sukhna, Mersa/Wadi Gawasis, Tell el-Dab'a) and quarries, not to speak of the impressive chain of fortresses built in northern Nubia.

As for royal palaces and their impact on the development of urban areas, the evidence is scarce (Lange-Athinodorou 2021). Pharaohs moved their capital to the north shortly after the country's reunification around 2050 BC and founded a brand new one at Itjtawy, a city not still excavated, though the tombs of kings and officials built nearby provide hints about its approximate location. Another case to consider is Tell Basta, in the central Delta. Archaeologists unearthed there the palace of a mayor that, in fact, is part of a royal palace covering about one hectare – one can compare it with the palatial complex of the governors of the oasis of Dakhla, dating from the late third millennium BC, that extended over 1,5 ha. The necropolis of the mayors and their families was built in its close vicinity, but no trace of a settlement dating back to the first half of the second millennium has been found there. Recent geomorphological research reveals that parts of the archaeological site of Tell Basta correspond to an ancient landscape of canals, with no sediments originating from a settlement (Lange-Athinodorou et al. 2019).

To conclude, I see that cities flourished in some areas of Egypt between 2160 and 1800 BC but remained modest in size and negligible as political actors. However, they became nodal points in the articulation of the territory and the circulation of commodities, a circumstance concomitant with the emergence of "citizens" and a "middle class" whose wealth was independent of services to the state. The increased relevance of cities is probably linked to the flows of exchanges crossing Nubia, Egypt and the surrounding desert areas to the Eastern Mediterranean and the Levant. Hence, the dispersal of cities across a relatively vast space – the navigating distance between Elephantine and the Mediterranean was about 1000 km – plus the heterogeneous structure of provincial powers prevalent there only exacerbated the marginal political role played by cities. They never represented a potential counter-power for kings and provincial nobles.

3.5 Informal Networks of Power

Egyptian officials loved boasting about the positions they held in the royal administration. Lists of titles and biographical statements about the missions they accomplished for the king figured prominently in their monuments and represented a source of pride and self-identity. Not by chance, one of the main goals of the monarchy after the reunification of the country aimed to reconstruct the administration and a hierarchical distribution of responsibilities and duties among different categories of governmental departments and dignitaries. The first corpus of literary texts dates precisely from this period and celebrates new values and an inspiring ethos addressed to the officials of a bureaucracy under reconstruction (Lichtheim 1988; Parkinson 1997, 2002; Quirke 2004a; Vernus 2010). Loyalty to the king and superiors, efficiency, protection of the poor and the weak and an ethic based on firm moral principles were supposed to guide their acts. However, the strings of administrative and honorific titles in the private monuments from this period convey an equivocal message. On the one hand, we are presented with the image of a country firmly held by an all-encompassing bureaucracy with well-defined functions and sustained by fluid channels of communication, so information, instructions and goods – both material and immaterial – circulated efficiently between deciders and simple scribes (Quirke 2004b). On the other hand, the idea of a well-regulated society, ready to obey and execute their sovereign's will immediately, expresses more an ideal than the reality of power. Thus, informal networks of power coexisted with the royal administration. Collaboration, negotiation, co-optation, favoritism, patronage and bribery (not to speak of utter corruption) were common practices that marked the limits and the possibilities in which the royal administration actually operated to run the country (Moreno García 2019: 87–136).

A literary composition that probably went back to this period was *The Teaching for (king) Merykare* (the first copies are dated somewhat later, about the 16th century BC), a sort of treaty about the realities and constraints in the exercise of royal power. Far from the ideal hierarchical worldview expressed in official monuments, it provides a unique alternative and more realistic view closer to the ground. Several statements stress the importance of rewards to get the support of officials and "great ones," that is to say, influential potentates, not necessarily members of the royal administration or the court. In the case of officials, the teaching advocates, for instance, *"respect the officials, make your people flourish"* and *"do not damage the officials on their seats of office"*, while the best attitude toward the "great ones" should be

> *enrich your great men, so they enact your laws. A man rich in his house will not take sides. The man who has no lack is the owner of goods. Poor people do not speak by their truth. One who says 'would that I had' is not just. He takes the side of his favourite. He sides with the lord of payments. The Great One, his great ones are great. A king lord of an entourage is a valiant (king). One rich in officials is the ennobled. May you say truth/justice in your house, that the officials who are on earth fear you"* and *"enrich your great ones, promote your (fighters?), make increase on the troops of your retinue, provide them with staff-lists, fixed with fields, secured with livestock.*

Finally, the text also suggests *don't expel a man from his father's property, don't reduce the nobles in their possessions* (Parkinson 1997: 212–234).

That the collaboration of influential people was indispensable for the monarchy to rule the country, so kings should reward and cherish them, was rarely recognized in official sources. The precedents can be traced back to an inscription of Khety II, a leader from Asyut who lived around 2050 BC, just before the reunification of Egypt: "you are generous to your beloved one(s). How glad are the great ones of your time, who became (great) because of your elevation!"

(El-Khadragy 2008: 226). The "great ones" (*ur*) were a category of potentates different from the "great ones" (*aa*) mentioned earlier (§3.3), as their political influence and status appear more relevant, covering provinces or regions, not localities. A text of the late second millennium BC evokes, for instance, a period of anarchy as a time when "the land of Egypt was in the hands of great ones and rulers of towns." Their local prominence emerges, for instance, on the occasion of ambitious royal building programs, when officials and localities provided workers, together with individuals whose personal names had a toponymical value and were used as synonyms of a district to indicate the geographical provenance of a team of workers (Andrássy 2009).

This points to the importance of patronage networks headed by local potentates and wealthy landholders. An excellent example is Heqanakhte, an affluent landowner who lived in the early second millennium BC. His correspondence reveals that at least eighteen people were part of his household, including his mother, his second wife, his son, two daughters, his older aunt or daughter, his youngest brother, his foreman (and this man's dependents), three farmers, and three female servants. Several documents record twenty-eight men with whom Heqanakhte had financial dealings. The most prestigious one was Herunefer, a high-status official addressed as Heqanakht's social superior who seems to have owned some fields in the same area in which Heqanakhte lived. Two other neighbors were relatively prosperous landowners too, who sold or leased substantial amounts of land to Heqanakhte. Finally, twenty-five people (also neighbors in some cases) owed him barley and emmer, including a governor of an agricultural center of the crown. Thus, the social network built around Heqanakhte included people from different social environments of higher, equal, and lower strata. Among these strata, a single person could simultaneously occupy different social positions. For example, one could at the same time be a subordinate of Heqanakhte while controlling other dependents, or (like Heqanakhte himself) a subordinate of Herunefer while also being the head of a substantial household. All the people mentioned could be roughly ascribed to the household proper as well as to an extended network of social relations (Allen 2002). The case of Heqanakhte was probably far from unique and points to a social sector of wealthy landholders who exerted a considerable influence over a territory. In their role as mediators, foremen or "entrepreneurs" who performed specialized services for high dignitaries, temples or the crown (for instance, by cultivating their fields), they represented a crucial link between the rural population, the royal administration and the high elite of the kingdom.

Local potentates acted as informal authorities in their territories. They also proved indispensable in mobilizing the workforce and resources the crown demanded. This fact provides another clue about the patronage networks celebrated in this time's private monuments and ritual compositions, for instance, in the tombs of wealthy provincial nobles that depict a myriad of people performing different tasks for their masters. In the case of the wealthiest households, they controlled hundreds of people. Only rarely do monuments and archaeology provide some information about the elusive world of wealthy people who did not belong to the categories of officials, provincial nobles and courtiers. Such is the case of "middle-class" owners of decorated stelae and cenotaphs built near the temple of Osiris at Abydos. Their lack of administrative titles suggests that their fortune did not derive from administrative positions, but they could afford nevertheless high-quality equipment to express their wealth and status (Moreno García 2019: 49–50, 169–171).

Did traders belong to this social category? Kings built numerous facilities to promote exchanges with foreign territories during the early second millennium BC. An extensive network of fortresses/emporia erected in northern Nubia, the harbors of Tell el-Dab'a (in the Eastern Delta), Mersa/Wadi Gawasis and Ayn Sukhna (in the Red Sea) leading to the Levant, Sinai and the southern Red Sea, respectively, and the commercial contacts with the Aegean, the Levant and Syria, attest to the importance of international trade. In some cases, provincial leaders promoted these contacts and apparently kept their own networks of contacts abroad, particularly those living in Middle Egypt. In other cases, trading activities were in the hands of people of lesser status (Moreno García 2017). Thus, the Nubian fortresses/emporia were surrounded by substantial non-fortified settlements, with Egyptian-style houses that included storage facilities (Knoblauch and Bestock 2014; Gratien and Miellé 2022). It is reasonable to assume that traders lived in these settlements and fortresses, built to promote exchanges and regularly visited by Nubian caravans that arrived there to trade (Liszka and Kraemer 2016). In the case of Tell el-Dab'a, this locality accommodated a multicultural society composed of Egyptian and Levantine traders, sailors, guides, soldiers and interpreters. Unfortunately, little is known about private merchants' activities, wealth and investments in the early second millennium BC. However, several localities were considered "gateways" to foreign territories. The officials in their charge supervised cargoes and caravans and, quite probably, collected taxes, as happened with the elites that controlled Middle Egypt. Not by chance, their tombs depict caravans of foreigners arriving into the Nile Valley as well as representations of Asian women and warriors (Figure 11) (Moreno García 2017).

The importance of trade in the early second millennium explains why harbors became conspicuous features in the settlement organization of the country. At the same time, individuals boasted about transporting goods and food on their initiative (Moreno García 2024). Several kinds of transactions reveal the importance of knowledge about relative value in the exchange system: The expanded

Figure 11 Asian caravan depicted in the tomb of Khnumhotep II at Beni Hasan (detail). Norman de Garis Davies, CC0, via Wikimedia Commons. https://commons.wikimedia.org/wiki/File:Leaders_of_the_Aamu_of_Shu_MET_DT272586.jpg

use of exchange values (like the *shenat*-unit) together with sealed documents and private seals; the introduction of the Egyptian word *menu/menet*, derived from the Mesopotamian *mina*-unit (about 500 grams), which came to mean "fixed amount," "share," and corresponded to the basic wages on which the Egyptian system of compensation rested; and the first appearance of a new title, "overseer of (exchange-)value" (Quirke 2004b: 68–69). A biographical account in the tomb of Sarenput I, governor of the caravan and harbor city of Elephantine around 1950 BC, epitomizes these transformations as he mentions control over river trade, harbors, markets and foreign commodities arriving into Egypt. He was "overseer of all tribute at the entrance of the foreign countries in the form of royal ornaments, to whom the tribute of the Medya-country was brought as a contribution of the rulers of the foreign countries", as well as "one who rejoices over the quay/market-place, the overseer of the great ships of the Royal Domain, who supplies the Double Treasury, the superior of the harbours in the province of Elephantine (so that) what navigates and what moors was under his authority" (Moreno García 2024).

3.6 The Interplay between Elites, Sub-elites and Informal Leaders

How did elites get along with other social groups holders of some authority? Official sources offer too much of an institutional view, in which the royal administration appears as the main arena of the legitimate interplay between officials, other elites, and common people, shaped by a hierarchical chain of command linking masters and subjects. Accordingly, initiative and command came from above, while deference, submission and diligence were expected from subjects (Gnirs 2000). The reality, however, was more nuanced because the monarchy's stability depended on its ability to harmonize the interests of different elite groups, arbitrate among them, and link their interests and perspectives to those of the monarchy itself. The distribution of material and immaterial goods served this purpose, from rewards and income to prestige and status. Specific "theaters of power" helped visualize the official who-is-who of the kingdom: The royal palace and its elaborated ceremonies, the rituals held at the royal funerary complexes, not to speak of temples, their hierarchical priestly bodies and their processions (Grajetzki 2009; Quirke 2018).

Nevertheless, official positions and ceremonial settings were also shaped by a complex set of social practices in which patronage, intrigue, favoritism, trust and bribery were as important – if not more – as efficiency and formal promotion. In other cases, such settings merely recognized the status of people whose sources of power were partially independent of the crown. For instance, when they came from powerful families well rooted in the provinces or the state apparatus for generations; or because their connections with the royal family and influential patrons gave them privileged access to the highest spheres of the kingdom. In other instances, influential people had no access to these ceremonial theatres despite their indispensable contribution to the stability of the kingdom and the effective implementation of royal orders. Village chiefs, wealthy peasants, rich traders, and powerful overseers, among others, likely belonged to this category but are poorly documented.

An important point is the absence of evidence about organized social bodies, holders of substantial executive power and autonomy outside the monarchy and its institutions, like assemblies of urban notables, guilds of merchants, priestly assemblies, or councils of elders capable of lobbying and influencing state initiatives. This means that the Egyptian organization of power remained essentially oligarchical, perhaps because the reduced size of cities and urban populations proved insufficient to generate influential bodies of this kind (Moreno García 2019; compare with Barjamovic and Yoffee 2020). This was also a period in which institutions later destined to provide alternative paths to wealth and power, like the army and the "colonial" administrators of the late second millennium BC, were much less significant too. In the end, the oligarchical organization of the monarchy means that the ideological emphasis on absolute royal power, sanctioned by the gods, may conceal other sources of social power, rarely referred to in the official record. To what extent these conditions contributed to eroding the cohesion of the elite and the authority of kings in the long term still awaits further analysis.

While some cities were economically important but politically irrelevant, other institutions played a crucial role as arenas where different social actors interplayed and obtained social recognition and wealth. Local temples were one of them. Access to their resources – land, cattle, offerings, workers, precious goods – provided income to local elites and sub-elites. Moreover, these institutions represented an ideal arena to connect the local elites with the monarchy – temples benefited from substantial royal grants of land and valuable equipment. However, the archaeological vestiges from this period suggest that temples had little in common with the massive architectural complexes and economic institutions of the late second millennium BC, like the Ramesseum or the temple of Amun at Karnak. On the contrary, provincial sanctuaries remained modest in size, although their assets could be considerable at the local scale. Some inscriptions from the 16th century BC reveal, for instance, that the temple of the goddess Nekhbet at Elkab controlled at least 1,400 arouras of land (385 ha) in this province, while the domain of god at Medamud (near Thebes) comprised 1,672 arouras (or 460 ha). As the total area of these provinces covered 22,500 and 28,400 ha, respectively, including marshes, settlements and pasture-land, these temples controlled a substantial part of their farmlands. This explains why temples remained the primary power basis of local elites who often struggled to monopolize the most prominent priestly positions and the income derived from them and the management of the gods' estates.

Therefore, the importance of provincial temples was such that it inspired a policy of selective royal donations of land, not to speak of their embellishment with high-quality ritual objects and works of art (statues, reliefs), including the erection of chapels intended to hold royal statues. The aim was to strengthen the links between the monarchy and the elite families that controlled the sanctuaries. The case of King Mentuhotep II, who reunified Egypt, is exemplary in this regard, because he contributed to the decoration of many temples in Upper Egypt at a time when the support from the leading families in this region was crucial for his political ambitions and the consolidation of his authority on Egypt (Grajetzki 2006: 20–21). As for modest priestly positions, they were usually reserved for minor branches of the ruling local family or members of the local sub-elites, thus tied to the leading families through patronage networks. Kings also built temples at important localities and, in the case of Thebes, they emphasized formal continuity with prestigious pharaohs of the past by erecting an "ancestor" chapel with statues that represented kings of the late third millennium BC and the founders of the Theban royal lineage, like Antef the Great (Lorand 2013).

The funerary complexes of the kings also provided occasions to strengthen the links between the most powerful families of the kingdom and the pharaohs. These complexes hosted towns inhabited by the ritual and administrative personnel in charge of the day-to-day management of these institutions, the provision of offerings and the performance of rituals. Ilahun and the "city" of Wah-sut at Abydos are the best preserved, and the positions they provided were usually reserved for high officials and provincial potentates (Wegner 2010). Some private monuments from this period record lists of many people, but the nature of their bonds remains obscure. Priestly positions figure prominently there, but not exclusively, so it may be possible that these monuments evoke informal "professional associations" that provided some support to their members or, simply, that people holding priestly positions had the resources and influence necessary to develop broad and influential social networks.

Another arena that facilitated collaboration between the administration and local elites and sub-elites was the organization and mobilization of workers to execute royal projects. Provincial leaders recruited hundreds of people employed as quarrymen, miners, builders, and even soldiers if required. Imeny, leader of Beni Hasan, claimed, for instance, that he took part in three missions for the king – a military expedition to Nubia and two mining missions at the head of 400 and 600 workers from his province (Lichtheim 1988: 138). In other cases, "mayors" accompanied the conscripts sent from their towns to the quarries, sometimes including hundreds of people. The inscriptions in the quarries of Hatnub or Wadi Hammamat provide factual information about such contingents, their supply and their organization. An example from Wadi Hammamat lists 17,000 conscripts accompanied by twenty "mayors." Another inscription from Thebes describes 3,000 men from several localities of the Theban province (Lichtheim 1988: 53). Mayors were also indispensable mediators for the crown, for instance, as tax collectors (Van den Boorn 1988). Thus, a scribe working for the temple of Elephantine around 1750–1650 BC claimed that he increased the taxes due to his master when the latter was deprived of "mayors" (Delange 1987: 220–223). Whereas the social background of many "mayors" and village chiefs is challenging to ascertain, the evidence suggests that they came from the local notables.

Activities like the daily management of the estates and households of landlords, nobles and dignitaries also put diverse sectors of Egyptian society into contact with each other. Administrators (lit. overseers of a house) were represented in the monuments of their masters, usually performing tasks such as monitoring the activities of peasants, herders and artisans. It is quite possible that many administrators were recruited from the upper sectors of rural society, like wealthy peasants and "mayors." For example, the composition of the teams of workers employed in the construction of royal pyramids and temples suggests that they were supervised by the leaders of their villages and districts, as can be inferred from the Reisner Papyri and the marks found in the pyramids at Lisht. In other cases, the geographical provenance of the workforce included the names of some managers followed by the hieroglyph meaning "locality," as if they were local potentates but not officials of the royal administration (Andrássy 2009). The correspondence of Heqanakhte, a wealthy landowner who lived in the early 20th century BC, also gives some clues about this social sector. Three men employed by Heqanakhte and put in charge of diverse agricultural tasks were designated as "farmers." The ambiguous Egyptian term employed (*ihwti*) refers both to modest farmers and wealthy peasants who cultivated the extensive landholdings of temples, high officials and nobles. Other administrators fulfilled the orders of the vizier, as in the case of several administrators in the Thinite province instructed to gather rowers, prepare cargoes and send provisions and workers. Many elite stelae inscribed between 2000–1800 BC enumerated not only the owners' family but also their subordinates, thus giving a clue about the composition of their households, which included their kin as well as farmers, servants, administrators and other personnel at their service. A capillary network of formal and informal social links thus connected the highest sectors of the society with the provincial elites and the rural sub-elites (Moreno García 2013; Grajetzki 2020).

A final point concerns the royal court as a meeting point for people from different social sectors. The papyrus Boulaq 18, an exceptional administrative document from the 18th century BC, records foodstuff deliveries to the personnel who frequented the Theban court for a few days. The primary beneficiaries were the royal family, high dignitaries, nobles and attendants. However, this document also refers to modest people who visited the royal palace for specific purposes, from farmers and people on missions to foreigners from the desert. These missions allowed them to meet people of higher status, become their employees, move into high society – for instance, as suppliers of goods and services – and join the elite patronage networks (e.g., Liszka 2023).

3.7 Royal Power, Its Limits and Weaknesses

The relatively brief period of reunification that began around 2050 BC and concluded slightly after 1800 BC is usually considered a time of cultural classicism, not only in visual and written arts but also for the Egyptian language. Nevertheless, the fact that the new pharaohs claimed royal continuity and the restoration of ancestral royal traditions barely conceals that a mere return to the previous monarchical order was impossible. The Theban kings who succeeded in reunifying Egypt struggled to consolidate their authority against firmly established interests and a fragile balance of power. They needed to display their political ability to have their rule accepted or, at least, tolerated by other powerful actors. If pyramids symbolized the capacity of kings to produce landscapes of power and memory centered on the monarchy in the third millennium BC, the apparent failure of the early second-millennium kings to achieve a similar goal reveals the difficulties they encountered. Royal pyramids were built, and courtiers and nobles were buried around them near Itjtawy, Egypt's new capital. However, they consisted of relatively modest, short-living complexes, far less attractive for the kingdom's elites than their predecessors at Saqqara, Giza or Abusir. Many officials, for instance, chose to be buried in the Theban necropoleis. What is more, some provincial nobles built massive tombs, almost royal in size, wealth and artistic splendor. Local leaders succeeded thus in accumulating substantial power and wealth and becoming simultaneously potential rivals as well as essential supporters of the monarchy.

Hence, the wealth that provincial nobles held, together with the existence of a sector of affluent people whose livelihoods were independent of any service to the state, suggest that the tax system was somewhat inefficient in capturing income and preventing the emergence of alternative nodes of wealth and power accumulation (Moreno García 2021). Finally, trade seems to be a significant enhancer in the organization of power in Egypt, and it may be possible that the very reunification of the country was finally the outcome of negotiations profitable for the whole political-commercial network involved, from the nobles of Middle Egypt to the local kings of remote Thebes. The latter were undoubtedly recognized as pharaohs of the entire country – provided they guaranteed the interests of other nodes of power in Egypt, like the nobles of Middle Egypt and, perhaps, Elephantine. The massive fortresses/factories built in Nubia, the increasing importance of the harbors of Tell el-Dab'a (Eastern Mediterranean) and Mersa/Wadi Gawasis (Red Sea), the strong presence of Levantine peoples in Egypt or the increasing contacts with the Aegean, Lebanon and northern Syria (particularly Ebla), attest the importance of such commercial interests. The Egyptian military and trading involvement in Nubia and the Levant, the mention of Nubian, Libyan and Levantine peoples in provincial inscriptions and ritual formulae (like the execration texts), not to mention literary compositions like *Sinuhe,* are the best expression of the importance of foreign exchange and contacts in this period (Moreno García 2017, 2021).

Far from the assumption that pharaohs enjoyed absolute power and uncontested authority, supported by an all-encompassing bureaucracy, the reality was more prosaic. The reunification of the country around 2050 BC by the Theban kings was possible through some agreement between pharaoh Mentuhotep II (2055–2004 BC) and key provincial nobles from Elephantine, Middle Egypt and the Eastern Delta, some of them loyal to Heracleopolis, the Theban rivals in the north. These nobles and their descendants rose to important positions in the new monarchy – including that of vizier – and provided specialists for managing the state. At the same time, they succeeded in preserving considerable autonomy. Shortly afterward, a vizier of possible provincial background, not linked to the royal family by blood ties, arrived on the throne of Egypt as Amenemhat I (1985–1956 BC). His reign was marked by turbulence: Armed conflict with an unspecified enemy until Amenemhat prevailed, helped by nobles from Middle Egypt; transfer of the capital from Thebes to the north, at Itjtawy, close to the Fayyum area, the core of the defeated Heracleopolitan kingdom; choice of this area as the new royal burial ground, far from the ancestral cemeteries situated in the Theban area; and his final murder in the course of a palace conspiracy. His son, Sesostris I (1956–1911 BC), provoked new rebellions in the south and established a system of coregency destined to last under his successors, an attempt to ensure that the transmission of royal power passed uncontested within the reigning family (Grajetzki 2006: 28–35).

These events reveal tensions among the ruling class related to the arrival on the throne of the first kings of the second millennium BC and perhaps as well to a significant structural problem inherited from the late third millennium BC that remained unsolved. Kings sought the support of elites from specific areas of Egypt, so the transfer of the capital from Thebes to the Fayyum area may reflect the latent hostility between pharaohs and the traditional Theban elites, as the latter may have felt somewhat displaced under the new monarchy. Elephantine and Middle Egypt (Beni Hasan, Bersheh, Asyut, Meir, Qaw el-Kebir) flourished, and leaders from these areas held important positions in the kingdom. They seem to have been involved in trade with foreign territories, at least at a scale unmatched by other provincial leaders. The new pharaohs deployed an intense involvement in foreign affairs, a move that benefited these local elites, who may have played a decisive role in orienting the royal policy abroad to fulfill their agendas. When the monarchy collapsed again in the early 18th century BC, trade and trading facilities remained operational and even flourished, as happened in some Nubian fortresses and with the harbors of Avaris/Tell el-Dab'a and Mersa/Wadi Gawasis. Another sign of royal vulnerability, this time in the domain of religious beliefs, may lie in the efforts of kings to link the monarchy to ritual landscapes centered not on their own tombs but on the cult of Osiris, whose temple at Abydos became a national pilgrimage center.

The monarchy appears thus somewhat fragile and unstable, based on oligarchic foundations and a system of wealth distribution not as favorable for its interests as it was in previous centuries. The emergence of literary compositions that celebrated order, loyalty and efficiency and denigrated the chaos provoked by the ruin of the monarchy seems a consequence of this situation. Other compositions and expressions celebrated the importance of the councils of dignitaries who advised the pharaoh, took decisions conjointly with him and promoted the new values cherished at the court: eloquence, decorum, discretion, sense of justice and piety (Parkinson 1997; Coulon 1999, 2002; Gnirs 2000; Quirke 2004a). When this monarchical order collapsed after 1800 BC, an overt oligarchical system of power was implemented instead, when people from a nonroyal background, as well as pharaohs issued from a limited set of noble families, came to the throne of an increasingly fragmented country (Quirke 1991b).

3.8 Immaterial Power: Law and Religious Rituals

Egyptian sources occasionally refer to law. However, there is no trace of any code or compilation of legal prescriptions until the first millennium BC. A pharaonic "Code of Hammurabi" is simply missing, as well as any mention of formal decisions taken by courts and judges based on specific corpus of laws. This circumstance may be the consequence of the cities' modest political role and the absence of effective civic counter-powers. In the case of Mesopotamia, for example, the involvement of urban notables in trade and commercial affairs – loans, sales, investments or joint ventures – influenced the configuration of power, especially in trading states centered on a main city like Ebla, Mari, Aššur, and others (Barjamovic 2018). When kings shared power with other political actors, when city assemblies influenced decision-making, laws may help regulate their interventions and interplay. However, very little in the known Mesopotamian laws of this period limits or even enables royal action (Richardson 2017).

The case of Egypt seems entirely different. Cities were modest in size, and while it is conceivable that merchants and artisans constituted a substantial social sector in some of them, they probably never represented more than a few dozen or, at most, hundreds of people in the largest settlements. The case of Elephantine, the caravan city located in southernmost Egypt, is a good example. The inscribed offering vessels placed in the tombs of the caravan leaders and other members of the local elite reveal that this group, who dominated Elephantine in the late third millennium BC, included only a few dozen people (Figure 12). Furthermore, Egyptian merchants and artisans, scattered across a myriad of small settlements over Egypt, probably never made up

Figure 12 View of Elephantine. David Stanley from Nanaimo, Canada, CC BY 2.0, <https://creativecommons.org/licenses/by/2.0>, via Wikimedia Commons. https://commons.wikimedia.org/wiki/File:Elephantine_Island_(8611294575).jpg

a homogeneous social group with clear and well-defined shared interests, capable of acting as a coherent group and exerting "national" political influence.

Quite the contrary, the recurrent periods of political division that fragmented Egypt resulted from the divergent interests between regions and the noble elites that ruled them. Lower Egypt was turned toward the Mediterranean, the Levant and the Near East, while Middle Egypt looked to the Levant and Nubia, and Thebes struggled to control exchanges across the Red Sea, the deserts, and the Nile, and gain access to Nubia. The shifting rivalries and alliances between these regional elites shaped the political arena, as the "reunification" wars reveal. Consequently, any "mercantile lobby," supported by urban assemblies and capable of coordinating actions across Egypt, seems a fiction. This may also explain the poor reputation that merchants enjoyed in ancient Egypt and their reluctance to present themselves as such in their monuments, so they remain practically invisible in the documentary and iconographic record. They may have preferred to present themselves under alternative identities such as priests and officials, more prestigious and better accepted socially (Moreno García 2019: 87–107).

The case of the elites of Middle Egypt in the early second millennium BC is exemplary in this regard. Judging from their titles, their wealth and status derived from control over overland trade and desert resources, but they hardly referred to these activities in their monuments. Only exceptional depictions of caravans, unusual epithets and titles ("he who loves myrrh," "overseer of priests to whom valuables are brought from foreign lands, (namely) myrrh and galena"), the reuse of archaic titles (like *miter*, related to desert tracks) and sparse biographical references to their activities abroad cast some light about the importance of control over trade and caravans in the territories they controlled. Kings may have felt compelled to support these nobles and their interests because the circulation of wealth they promoted benefited the monarchy too. As early as Mentuhotep II's reign, the king travelled to Elephantine with his treasurers and two nobles, one from Meir in Middle Egypt, the other from the Eastern Delta, to oversee the arrival of ships from Nubia (Petrie 1888: plate 8). Kings in subsequent years invested considerable resources to build a chain of fortified trading posts around the Second Cataract of the Nile to control Nubian trade. In any case, kings could shift their support from some regions and sectors of the elite to others to get a balance of power more favorable for their interests and curtail any potential challenge. However, the undesirable corollary was to strengthen the power of some local nobles even more and thereby weaken the crown's political support.

Therefore, contrary to some views about the importance of "law," "judges," and "judicial departments" in ancient Egypt, clear evidence about them is actually surprisingly rare. Courts usually consisted of ad hoc meetings of people invested with authority, primarily agents of the king (scribes, high dignitaries, officials), temple personnel and potentates. These persons had access to archives and were capable of invoking precedents. They took into account local practices and customs in their decisions, but they were not "professional," full-time judges. In the absence of bodies of laws and formal regulations, the crown's agents enjoyed considerable autonomy, including the capacity to abuse their authority. In this context, crown agents, influential dignitaries and local potentates may have imposed their decisions easily, the only limit being other officials or vague allusions to moral principles and subordination to superiors.

The pleas of the famous *Eloquent Peasant* are a good literary illustration of such practices (Gnirs 2000), but administrative documents from all periods, such as the trial of Mose, the late New Kingdom tomb robberies or the conflicts evoked in papyrus Rylands 9, reveal that formal "legal" procedures were not exempted from abuse, bribery and utter corruption when put into practice. Therefore, references to "law" in ancient Egyptian sources, at least prior to the first millennium BC, may refer to a mix of former royal decisions, customary traditions, proper procedure, written or remembered precedents, moral behavior and ethical values or mere common sense. Even in the case of royal decisions enacted through royal decrees, they were often fragile, their observance far from guaranteed and frequently ignored by the officials in charge of their observance. As a result, some royal decrees included detailed descriptions of the severe punishments imposed on negligent and corrupt officials. In the end, "law" hardly provided a basis for the regulation of conflicts and to inspire an open, nonarbitrary interplay between different actors, favoring the emergence of a "public sphere," or to guarantee political deliberation able to influence decision-making (Moreno García 2019: 114–116).

As for temples, previous interpretations – and modern popular culture – saw these institutions as a potential menace for the monarchy as holders of substantial wealth thanks to royal endowments and private donations. Hence, priests would have accumulated considerable resources and, consequently, power and social and political influence to the detriment of the monarchy. However, this view has been gradually abandoned. Egyptian priesthood was frequently a part-time occupation, so dignitaries and officials, from military personnel to scribes and administrators, held ritual positions in temples alongside their current "secular" functions. Furthermore, temples were also controlled by the monarchy, subject to taxes and the revocation of temporal privileges and exemptions. At the same time, their goods remained at the disposal of the crown when needed and the kings embellished and rebuilt temples across Egypt (including the erection of chapels with royal statues), appointed and dismissed priests and ritualists, and granted land, revenue and remunerated positions to selected officials, thus interfering in the autonomy of these institutions. In practice, the limits between temples and other institutions of the monarchy remained frequently blurred, so it seems more appropriate to consider temples as autonomous specialized institutions subject nevertheless to royal interventions when required. In the late second millennium BC, for instance, temples administered crown land, even the fields of other temples, according to an indirect managerial system that helped the monarchy and sanctuaries reduce expenses. The crown rewarded officials and nobles with temple land and priestly positions, so these crossed interests helped the elites side with the monarchy. Nevertheless, this circumstance offered the local elites a substantial basis of power and wealth that they used to consolidate their local ascendancy and project their ambitions into a broader "national" sphere, like the royal court or the ruling circles of the palace. Texts from different periods confirm that local elites succeeded in controlling the sanctuaries in their territories for generations and that access to these institutions and their economic assets was fiercely restricted. It was not rare that violent episodes erupted from time to time, such as the dozens of people massacred at the temple of Mendes in the late third millennium BC or the conflict recorded in the papyrus Rylands 9 during the mid-first millennium BC. Finally, local cults were crucial to forging local identities, expressed through concepts like "city god" or by anthroponyms composed with the names of such divinities.

Temples were far from being cult centers open to any believer, like modern churches, mosques or synagogues. Even in the case of the more important sanctuaries, the massive walls marked a net distinction between "inside" and "outside," between people with and without access to their installations. Even some areas within temple enclosures were used as residential areas (some examples: Kemp 2004; Lehner 2015; Masson-Berghoff 2021). Similar conditions prevailed in small provincial sanctuaries. Given the oligarchical nature of Egyptian power, the temples remained in the hands of the elite, both "national" and local, and played a crucial role in preserving their wealth, status and influence – all the more so during recurrent periods of monarchical collapse. In the absence of clearly defined laws and judicial powers capable of enforcing them, temples remained instruments of order and institutional security for the elite, even to validate commercial transactions. Hence, private land donations to sanctuaries probably obeyed a strategy of partial property transfers, thus put safely under the protection of a divinity – donors usually controlled the land donated either as administrators or priests. In all, temples cannot be seen as independent actors but as tools in the hands of the ruling elite of ancient Egypt. They provided the ideological, economic and political basis to preserve and, subsequently, rebuild either statehood or the status of the elite, so their fate was closely linked to that of kings and nobles, not to popular devotion (Moreno García 2019).

3.9 Immaterial Power: Written Culture

Writing appeared in Egypt in the second half of the fourth millennium BC, but the first "literary" compositions only date from the early second millennium BC. Perhaps this was due to the absence of a public sphere in which political persuasion, collective forms of reflection expressed and transmitted in specific cultural ways, and even political thought, were encoded in any particular written genre, produced – or not – by a scribal class. Only at such a point could diverse actors sharing the same cultural values "consume" the resulting productions. Egypt hardly exhibited any of these characteristics. Contrary to Mesopotamia, writing emerged primarily to celebrate kings and preserve their names, deeds and relations with the tutelary divinities that protected pharaohs and, through their mediation, Egypt and its people. Hence, from its very beginning, writing was closely linked to the palatial sphere, not to cities or specific socio-political groups unrelated to the crown. Later on, writing spread across the country but was only accessible – apparently – to the elite and the scribes who formed the backbone of the royal administration. In such a vertical and centralized cultural and political order, there was little room for elaborated written expressions celebrating alternative points of view, like personal reflections about power or society, collections of maxims, or literary compositions in which ordinary people expressed their values, concerns, and aspirations. That those hypothetical expressions might find a social echo that helped create shared values and a sociocultural imaginary was simply inconceivable.

Two corpora of early compositions did escape from mere utilitarianism's narrow margins; still, both were closely related to the monarchy's needs and represented achieved manifestations of the palatial values. The first set of early compositions consisted of compilations of funerary formulae inscribed in the inner walls of the royal pyramids. The so-called Pyramid Texts prepared the king for his afterlife and contained detailed descriptions of his relations with the gods. The second one comprised the (auto)biographies inscribed on the monuments of scribes, local nobles and high dignitaries during the second half of the third millennium BC. They were highly formalized and hardly mentioned private matters and personal concerns. On the contrary, they mentioned exceptional events or a set of events in the life of an individual that deserved the king's praise before the court, or, as it happened more frequently since 2300 BC, described the progress of an official's career. These events proved the moral qualities, administrative diligence and excellent behavior of the protagonist, in perfect agreement with the ideals of order, hierarchy and good rule embodied by the king and his officials (Lichtheim 1988; Stauder-Porchet, Frood, and Stauder 2020). The rich iconography that decorated many private tombs of the third millennium BC also replicated these same ideals in the visual sphere. The so-called "scenes of everyday life," with their colorful representations of people and officials engaged in their ordinary occupations, from agriculture to hunting, conveyed an ideal of prosperity, order and hierarchy in which everyone had a defined place assigned and a task to perform. Biographies were thus a product of the palatial sphere and the values that legitimized and justified its rule.

The end of the unified monarchy around 2160 BC had the potential to open new scenarios in which writing might escape from the narrow limits of the palatial culture and, in doing so, explore fresh ways to encode unofficial personal and collective reflections. However, power did not become more "democratic." Provincial nobles and warlords still dominated the political sphere between 2160 and 2050 BC. Cities and their inhabitants did rise to a more prominent role, but they failed to become a counter-power or impose a distinctive cultural agenda (Moreno García 2024). The weight of tradition and the failure to develop a public sphere may explain why the old palatial culture continued to fix the frames (genres, textual structure, themes, values) in which subsequent compositions were written. Biographies reproduced the compositional structure established in the late third millennium and only included a few new expressions emphasizing individual agency, for instance, that individuals had accumulated wealth by their acts and protected the house of their ancestors. As for the Pyramid Texts, they expanded and entered into the private sphere because they were now used to guide individuals, and not only royals, into the afterlife. Nevertheless, far from expressing popular religiosity, these expanded compositions – known as Coffin Texts – remained restricted to nobles, dignitaries and their families.

Furthermore, while officials circulated between the royal courts of Heracleopolis and Thebes during Egypt's reunification around 2050 BC, they failed to inspire a "Confucian moment" and reflect on the nature of power, the fragility of kingship and the possibility of a renewed "social pact" between rulers and ruled based on *civic virtues*, not merely on absolute authority (Moreno García 2019: 153–154). This circumstance is particularly striking because cities increased their economic importance during this time. However, the expansion of cities and cadres of officials/scholars did not create a public sphere, to broaden discussions on collective matters and create a public receptive to new ideas. Some compositions like *The Teaching for (king) Merykare*, *The Loyalist Teaching* or *The Dialogue between a Man and his Soul* suggest that authors explored these possibilities nevertheless. In any case, the reunification of Egypt under a single monarch around 2050 BC and the return to a centralized power structure halted such an intellectual trend.

Hence, the development of the first "literary" compositions shortly after the reunification of Egypt remained constricted within the cultural limits established by the monarchy. The Theban rulers who succeeded in reunifying Egypt faced a formidable task: rebuilding the administration, co-opting leaders from the newly conquered regions, implementing a tax system, recruiting a new scribal class and inspiring loyalty toward the new pharaohs (Figure 13). The changes in the balance of power that occurred since 2160 meant that a simple return to the old administrative model operative between 2350 and 2160 BC was no longer possible. So, an innovative set of written compositions instilled the official values promoted by the monarchy: order, efficiency, loyalty, justice, hierarchy and moral behavior. They fell into three main genres: Teachings intended to educate scribes and dignitaries-to-be into the new ideals cherished by the monarchy; "pessimistic" texts that described the consequences of the

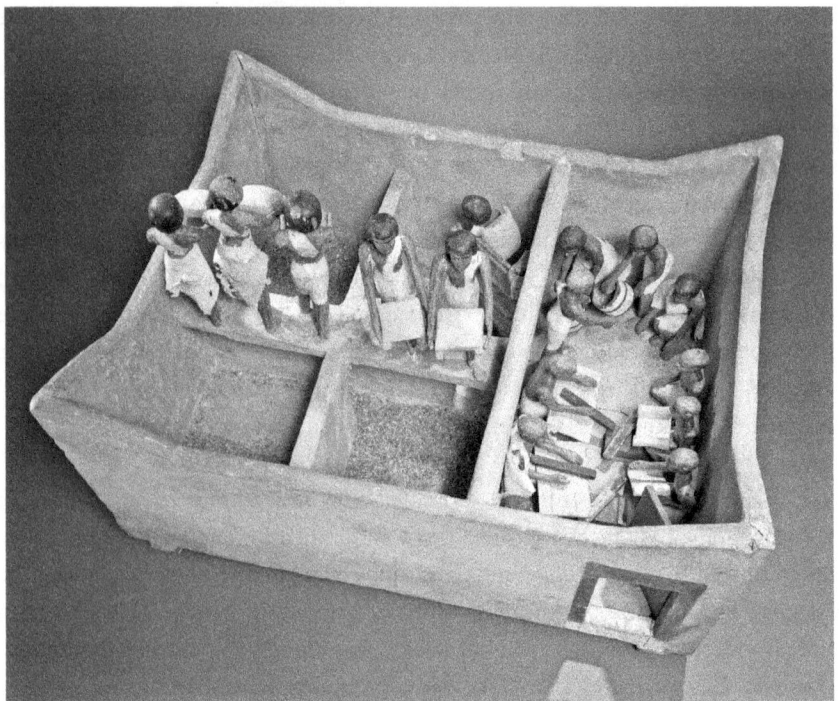

Figure 13 Scribes overseeing a granary. Metropolitan Museum of Art, CC0, via Wikimedia Commons. https://commons.wikimedia.org/wiki/File: Model_of_a_Granary_with_Scribes_MET_DP351558.jpg

absence of kings and the order they kept; and, finally, narrative tales in which adversities only strengthened the moral values and exemplary behavior of their protagonists until justice prevailed finally again, as in *The Eloquent Peasant* or *The Tale of Sinuhe* (Parkinson 1997, 2002; Quirke 2004a).

However, the decades following the end of the monarchy, from 2160 BC on, also witnessed the emergence of new *private* values that owed nothing to the monarchy and its cultural codes: self-confidence, acting by oneself, private wealth acquisition or preservation of the ancestral house. At the same time, the use of writing expanded in the private sphere, mainly in letters (as with "letters to the dead"), sealed agreements in everyday transactions (Moreno García 1997: 1–90), and the formation of private libraries that included non-canonical literary compositions and literary-religious texts (Quirke 2016). In light of this evidence, one can wonder if writing could in fact express these alternative, private values in elaborated compositions that might circulate and reach a broad public without the consent or control of the scribal class. There are only glimpses of such a possibility.

An intriguing text, the *Dialogue Between a Man and His Soul*, describes the personal distress of a priest and his experience of a dismaying reality. As Parkinson stated, "the inability of past speech to express the sage's present agony takes on a new dimension, as he laments that evil is so pervasive that the past is no longer a model that can be imitated" (Parkinson 1997: 144). That the story was set in the so-called golden era of the early second millennium BC and that his complaint is not addressed to a particular authority but to his own heart – thus kept in the private sphere – points to a skeptical view about the royal rule, even in a reunified country, and the hope of a better life after death. Another intriguing composition, *The Teaching for (king) Merykare*, was framed as the confrontation of a king-to-be with the realities of power in somewhat realistic terms. The composition does not hesitate to evoke past mistakes and the need to get the loyalty of nobles and courtiers through abundant rewards. In all, it instills a certain disillusionment into the exercise of power. It mentions the pernicious influence of demagogues capable of luring urban audiences into rebellion, as if "citizens" had the potential to challenge royal authority and take political initiatives. Finally, *The Loyalist Teaching* text advocates loyalty to the king but also caring for ordinary people, because "it is mankind who create all that exists, one lives on what comes from their hands; they are lacking, and then poverty prevails, the professions are what provide provisions" and "fight for men in every respect; they are a flock, good for their lord" (Parkinson 1997: 240–241). Frank statements like these about the importance of ordinary people are unusual in Egyptian texts. They express a sort of "social deal" in which the importance of both kings and commoners is recognized and, consequently, reciprocity exhorted.

Therefore, compositions such as The *Dialogue of a Man with His Soul* or *The Teaching for (King) Merykare* suggest a more critical attitude about using the past as a guide for action, particularly when compared to the official culture and its emphasis on tradition and repeated enactment of royal actions that helped reproduce social order. They may even suggest that some sectors of the learned class showed skepticism about the traditional values and beliefs they were supposed to embody, thus pointing to a certain intellectual autonomy.

4 Conclusions

In the preceding pages, we have focused mainly on the Old Babylonian period (2004–1595 BC) and the Egyptian First Intermediate Period, and the Middle Kingdom (2160–1750 BC), roughly a 400-year stretch of time during which the political landscape was occasionally fragmented, and the control of various states over places and dimensions of socio-economic life was often incomplete. Partly as a consequence, we have paid attention to the many ways in which ancient states did not work, or did not work *well*, or as well as they said they did. This inflects our discussion in two basic ways. First, a multi-polity political culture was the norm for Mesopotamia, and unified states were the exception (much as it was in ancient Greece) while, in the Egyptian case, unification was not necessarily the ultimate nor the most desirable political goal; second, Egyptian and Mesopotamian states exercised limited infrastructural powers (of law, citizenship, taxation, etc.) despite claims to greater ones. Both the extensivity and intensity of state power were thus relatively low. What this does not imply (as sometimes is made to seem the necessary sequela) is that because state power was low, other forms of institutional power must have had a larger share of the pie: that local authorities, powerful families, temples, the army, merchants, officials, and so on, must have held the kinds of authorities not exercised by states. Studies have argued for the robust authority of city assemblies, demonstrated that official positions were held in family lines for multiple generations, or that temple organizations were durable and modular institutions parallel rather than subsidiary to states. Though instances of each can be demonstrated, raising them to categorical importance assumes a priori the pie-ness of power: that state societies always exist with {X} critical mass of power, and that the task of historians is therefore to determine the percentage held by different sectors and actors in order to understand the whole – that weak states must mean strong temples/families/officials, and vice-versa.

Our opinion is rather different. We see states which were weak, but in a balance of low power with *other* weak civic/social institutions. Despite historical periods or instances in which we can discern instances of "local power," the cases are too disparate and particular to be convincing that they were systematically counterweights to the state. This was a world with an underdeveloped civil society; where economic inequality was relatively low and financial institutions virtually nonexistent; where constraints of technology, communication, and distance limited aggregations of power of all kinds, state and otherwise; where "aristocracies," if any, were limited to particular areas inside kingdoms. Low power generalized across all levels and sectors of society seems not only more plausible than its hoarding in any one place, but also the situation that the evidence actually demonstrates: a homology of generalized weakness. As much economic or social power as an Ur-Utu or a Heqanakhte ever had, it only ever extended as far as a large household or a local territory. They had neither the ability nor the interest to create the kinds of durable symbols of power that states and institutions could (e.g., monuments or literary works), nothing to transcend the times and places in which they lived.

What should fascinate us is that the range of institutions and actors we see still acted, interacted, and generated stable political, economic, and social systems with only low amounts of raw power: This is a "positive" weakness perhaps to be celebrated rather than deplored. Suppose we do not see individual instances of state or local power as indicative of absolute capacity. In that case, we see them as efforts to exercise, attain, or bring about the kinds of capacities they gesture toward. Massive claims in the ideological sphere may thus correspond, in reality, to the limited capacities of political agency. Thus, rather than a pie to cut up, we think of a young forest in which institutions – including the state – were like young and resilient trees, which might or might not grow larger, or come to be supplanted by second-growth species.

Early states were thus similar to their later modern cousins in form but not scale or (therefore) kind; each was an entity within a field of similar institutions, connected but distinct. This précis frames the Mesopotamian and Egyptian "organization of power" we have presented. Not every Assyriologist or Egyptologist will agree with our analysis. Especially those who study the *Hauptreichen* and empires of Akkad, Ur III, Neo-Assyria, and Neo-Babylonia – altogether comprising about 550 out of the 3,000 years of the political tradition we study here –, not to speak the Egyptian Kingdoms/Empires – like the Old, Middle, and New Kingdoms – may less well recognize the low-power model we outline here. That is only as it should be: for some periods of their history, Mesopotamian and Egyptian states were able to aggregate political power more extensively and intensively than was usually the case. We may freely recognize that this was the case without adverting to the notion that exceptions are rules. We also express our discomfort with the outlines of Egyptian and Mesopotamian history originally elaborated in the 19th and early 20th centuries AD, when the European experience was regarded as the superior standard to be imitated by any other polity. The notion of *state* was central in this period when nation-states were struggling to be born and consolidate themselves. Other alternative forms were disregarded under categories such as "tributary state," "tribal societies," and "chiefdoms," which allegedly exhibited features quite opposed to those prevailing in Europe and North America. Inversely, ancient long-lived or sophisticated states should replicate in one way or another the characteristics ascribed to modern, "advanced" states, so ancient sources were read and interpreted under this lens: bureaucratic organization, centralization, even urbanism and rationality preceded the forms that would finally blossom in Europe and North America. If one adds the influence of art history (sophisticated art = centralization; poor art = decadence), the consequences still dominate current interpretations of, say, Egypt's Middle Kingdom or Ur III Mesopotamia, and the importance ascribed to classical Egyptian literature or the code of Hammurabi as proof of successful political centralization and ordered rule.

Luckily, increasing research in other regions of the world, like pre-colonial Africa or pre-Columbian America, reveals a plethora of forms of political organization that surpass the narrow limits based on the Western experience. The considerable wealth of information thus gathered helps to rethink former interpretations, re-read ancient sources, integrate written and archaeological data and enrich the definition of basic concepts from "city" to "state." If readers may find this book a valuable step in this direction, our effort will be largely fulfilled.

References

Abed, B. (2018). *The Royal Archive of the King Iluni from Basi City*. Baghdad.

Adams, R. McC. (1981). *Heartland of Cities: Surveys of Ancient Settlement and Land Use on the Central Floodplain of the Euphrates*. Chicago: The University of Chicago Press.

Adams, R. McC. (2009). Old Babylonian Networks of Urban Notables. *Cuneiform Digital Library Journal*. **2009**(7), 1–14. https://cdli.ucla.edu/pubs/cdlj/2010/cdlj2010_002.html.

Adams, R. McC., and Kraeling, C. H., eds. (1960). *City Invincible: A Symposium on Urbanization and Cultural Development in the Ancient Near East*. Chicago: The University of Chicago Press.

Allen, J. P. (2002). *The Heqanakht Papyri*. New York: The Metropolitan Museum of Art.

Andrássy, P. (2009). Symbols in the Reisner Papyri. In P. Andrássy et al., eds., *Non-textual Marking Systems, Writing and Pseudo Script from Prehistory to Modern Times*. Göttingen: Seminar für Ägyptologie und Koptologie, pp. 113–122.

Bahrani, Z. (2006). Race and Ethnicity in Mesopotamian Antiquity. *World Archaeology*, **38**(1), 48–59.

Baines, J., and Yoffee, N. (1998). Order, Legitimacy, and Wealth in Ancient Egypt and Mesopotamia. In G. M. Feinman, and J. Marcus, eds., *Archaic States*. Santa Fe: School of American Research Press, pp. 199–260.

Bang, P., and Scheidel, W., eds. (2013). *The Oxford Handbook of the State in the Ancient Near East and Mediterranean*. Oxford: Oxford University Press.

Barjamovic, G. (2004). Civic Institutions and Self-Government in Southern Mesopotamia in the Mid-First Millennium BC. In J. G. Dercksen, ed., *Assyria and Beyond: Studies Presented to Mogens Trolle Larsen*. Leiden: Nederlands Instituut voor het Nabije Oosten, pp. 47–98.

Barjamovic, G. (2018). Interlocking Commercial Networks and the Infrastructure of Trade in Western Asia during the Bronze Age. In K. Kristiansen, Th. Lindkvist, and J. Myrdal, eds., *Trade and Civilization: Economic Networks and Cultural Ties, from Prehistory to the Early Modern Era*. Cambridge: Cambridge University Press, pp. 113–142.

Barjamovic, G., and Yoffee, N. (2020). Working at Home, Travelling Abroad: Old Assyrian Trade and Archaeological Theory. In J. Mas, and P. Notizia, eds., *Working at Home in the Ancient Near East*. Oxford: Archaeopress, pp. 107–116.

Bauer, J. Englund, R. K., and Krebernik, M. (1998). *Mesopotamien: Späturuk-Zeit und Frühdynastische Zeit*. Freiburg-Göttingen: Universitätsverlag/Vandenhoeck und Ruprecht.

Beaulieu, P.-A. (2017). Palaces of Babylon and Palaces of Babylonian Kings. *Journal of the Canadian Society for Mesopotamian Studies*, **11–12**, 5–14.

Bietak, M. (2018). The Many Ethnicities in Avaris: Evidence from the Northern Borderland of Egypt. In J. Budka, and J. Auenmüller, eds., *From Microcosm to Macrocosm: Individual Households and Cities in Ancient Egypt and Nubia*. Leiden: Sidestone Press, pp. 73–92.

Charpin, D. (1981). La Babylonie de Samsu-iluna à la Lumière de Nouveaux Documents. *Bibliotheca Orientalis*, **38**, 517–547.

Charpin, D., Edzard, D. O., and Stol, M. (2004). *Mesopotamien: die altbabylonische Zeit*. Freiburg-Göttingen: Universitätsverlag/Vandenhoeck und Ruprecht.

Coulon, L. (1999). La Rhétorique et ses Fictions: Pouvoirs et Duplicité du Discours à travers la Littérature Égyptienne du Moyen et du Nouvel Empire. *Bulletin de l'Institut Français d'Archéologie Orientale*, **99**, 103–132.

Coulon, L. (2002). Cour, courtisans et modèles éducatifs au Moyen Empire. *Egypte, Afrique et Orient* 26, 2002, 9–20.

Dahl, J. L. (2006). Review of Sharlach 2004. *Journal of the American Oriental Society*, **126**, 77–88.

De Graef, K. (1999a). Les Étrangers dans les Textes Paléobabyloniens Tardifs de Sippar. *Akkadica*, **111**, 1–48.

De Graef, K. (1999b). Les Étrangers dans les Textes Paléobabyloniens Tardifs de Sippar. *Akkadica*, **112**, 1–17.

Delange, E. (1987). *Catalogue des Statues Égyptiennes du Moyen Empire 2060–1560 avant J.-C.* Paris: Réunion des Musées Nationaux.

Diego Espinel, A. (2019). "Unusual Herders": Iconographic Development, Diffusion and Meanings of Dwarves, Boys and Lame and Emaciated People as Drovers from the Old Kingdom to the Early Middle Kingdom. In P. Piacentini, and A. D. Castelli, eds., *Old Kingdom Art and Archaeology 7: Proceedings of the International Conference Università degli Studi di Milano 3–7 July 2017*. Milan: Università degli Studi di Milano, pp. 418–435.

Eidem, J. (2010). *The Royal Archives from Tell Leilan: Old Babylonian Letters and Treaties from the Eastern Lower Town Palace*. Leiden: Nederlands Instituut voor het Nabije Oosten.

El-Khadragy, M. (2008). The Decoration of the Rock-Cut Chapel of Khety II at Asyut. *Studien zur Altägyptischen Kultur*, **37**, 219–241.

Eyre, Ch. (2013). *The Use of Documents in Pharaonic Egypt*. Oxford: Oxford University Press.

Farout, D. (2009). Isi, un Saint Intercesseur à Edfou. *Égypte, Afrique et Orient*, **53**, 3–10.

Forstner-Müller, I. (2021). Central Power and the Harbour: Some Thoughts on the Main Harbour of Avaris in the Middle Kingdom and Second Intermediate Period. In A. Tenu, and M. Yoyotte, eds., *Le roi et le fleuve. Exemples d'usages pluriels de l'espace*. Paris: Éditions Khéops, pp. 109–123.

Franke, D. (1994). *Das Heiligtum des Heqaib auf Elephantine*. Heidelberg: Heidelberger Orientverlag.

Garfinkle, S. (2007). Public versus Private in the Ancient Near East. In D. Snell, ed., *A Companion to the Ancient Near East*. Oxford: Wiley-Blackwell, pp. 384–396.

Garfinkle, S. (2012). *Entrepeneurs and Enterprise in Early Mesopotamia: A Study of Three Archives from the Third Dynasty of Ur*. Bethesda: CDL Press.

Gibson, McG., and Biggs, R. D., eds. (1991). *The Organization of Power: Aspects of Bureaucracy in the Ancient Near East*. Chicago: The Oriental Institute of the University of Chicago.

Gnirs, A., ed. (2000). *Reading the Eloquent Peasant*. Hamburg: Widmeier Verlag.

Grajetzki, W. (2006). *The Middle Kingdom of Ancient Egypt: History, Archaeology and Society*. London: Gerald Duckworth.

Grajetzki, W. (2009). *Court Officials of the Egyptian Middle Kingdom*. London: Bristol Classical Press.

Grajetzki, W. (2020). *The People of the Cobra Province in Egypt: A Local History, 4500 to 1500 BC*. Oxford: Oxbow Books.

Gratien, B., and Miellé, L. (2022). *Mirgissa VI: La Ville hors les Murs*. Cairo: Institut Français d'Archéologie Orientale.

Harris, R. (1975). *Ancient Sippar: A Demographic Study of an Old Babylonian City (1894–1595 BC)*. Leiden: Nederlands Instituut voor het Nabije Oosten.

Ilin-Tomich, A. (2017). Regional Administration in Late Middle Kingdom Egypt. In M. Tomorad, and J. Popielska-Grzybowska, eds., *Egypt 2015: Perspectives of Research. Proceedings of the Seventh European Conference of Egyptologists*. Oxford: Archaeopress, pp. 307–318.

Janssen, C. (2022). Thirteen Bones and a Skeleton: The Location of Inanna-mansum's Grave and Material Manifestations of the Cult of the Dead in Old Babylonian Sippar. *Akkadica*, **143**(1), 59–100.

Joannès, F. (2006). *Haradum II: Les textes de la Période Paléo-babylonienne*. Paris: Éditions recherche sur les civilisations.

Kemp, B. J. (2004). The First Millennium BC: Temple Enclosure or Urban Citadel? *Cambridge Archaeological Journal*, **14**(2), 271–276.

Knoblauch, C., and Bestock, L. (2014). The Uronarti Regional Archaeological Project: Final Report of the 2012 Survey. *Mitteilungen des Deutschen Archäologischen Instituts*, **69**, 103–142.

Lange-Athinodorou, E. (2021). The Issue of Residence and Periphery in the Middle Kingdom: Surveying the Delta. In A. Jiménez Serrano, and A. J. Morales, eds., *Middle Kingdom Palace Culture and Its Echoes in the Provinces*. Leiden: Brill, pp. 256–283.

Lange-Athinodorou, E. Abd El-Raouf, A., Ullmann, T., Trappe, J., Meister, J. and Baumhauer, R. (2019). The Sacred Canals of the Temple of Bastet at Bubastis (Egypt): New Findings from Geomorphological Investigations and Electrical Resistivity Tomography (ERT). *Journal of Archaeological Science: Reports*, **26**. https://doi.org/10.1016/j.jasrep.2019.101910.

Lehner, M. (2015). Shareholders: The Menkaure Valley Temple Occupation in Context. In P. Der Manuelian, and Th. Schneider, eds., *Towards a New History for the Egyptian Old Kingdom: Perspectives on the Pyramid Age*. Leiden: Brill, pp. 227–314.

Lichtheim, M. (1988). *Ancient Egyptian Autobiographies Chiefly of the Middle Kingdom: A Study and an Anthology*. Freiburg-Göttingen: Universitätsverlag/ Vandenhoeck Ruprecht.

Liszka, K. (2023). Eight Medjay Walk into a Palace: Bureaucratic Categorization and Cultural Mistranslation of Peoples in Contact. In D. Candelora, N. Ben-Marzouk, and K. Cooney, eds., *Ancient Egyptian Society: Challenging Assumptions, Exploring Approaches*. London: Routledge, pp. 122–139.

Liszka, K., and Kraemer, B. (2016). Evidence for Administration of the Nubian Fortresses in the Late Middle Kingdom: P. Ramesseum 18. *Journal of Egyptian History*, **9**, 151–208.

Liverani, M. (1996). Reconstructing the Rural Landscape of the Ancient Near East. *Journal of the Economic and Social History of the Orient*, **39**, 1–41.

Liverani, M. (1999). The Role of the Village in Shaping the Ancient Near Eastern Rural Landscape. In L. Milano, S. de Martino, F. M. Fales, and G. B. Lanfranchi, eds., *Landscapes: Territories, Frontiers and Horizons in the Ancient Near East, Part I: Invited Lectures*. Padua: Sargon Press, pp. 37–48.

Liverani, M. (2014). The King and His Audience. In S. Gaspa, A. Greco, D. Morandi Bonacossi, S. Ponchia, and R. Rollinger, eds., *From Source to History: Studies on Ancient Near Eastern Worlds and Beyond*. Münster: Ugarit Verlag, pp. 373–385.

Lorand, D. (2013). Une "Chapelle des Ancêtres" à Karnak sous Sésostris Ier? *Cahiers de Karnak*, **14**, 447–466.

Macginnis, J. (2012). Evidence for a Peripheral Language in a Neo-Assyrian Tablet from the Governor's Palace in Tušhan. *Journal of Near Eastern Studies*, **71**(1), 13–20.

Małecka-Drozd, N. (2021). Nile Delta Settlements during the Early Dynastic and Old Kingdom Periods – Their Internal Structure, Variability, and Evidence of "Royal" Influence. *Ägypten und Levante*, **31**, 301–338.

Masson-Berghoff, A. (2021). *Le Quartier des Prêtres dans le Temple d'Amon à Karnak*. Leuven: Peeters.

Moeller, N. (2016). *The Archaeology of Urbanism in Ancient Egypt: From the Predynastic Period to the End of the Middle Kingdom*. Cambridge: Cambridge University Press.

Moeller, N. (2023). Urban versus Village Society in Ancient Egypt: A New Perspective. In D. Candelora, N. Ben-Marzouk, and K. M. Cooney, eds., *Ancient Egyptian Society: Challenging Assumptions, Exploring Approaches*. London: Routledge, pp. 248–264.

Moreno García, J. C. (1997). *Études sur l'administration, le pouvoir et l'idéologie en Égypte, de l'Ancien au Moyen Empire*. Liège: Centre Informatique de Philosophie et Lettres.

Moreno García, J. C. (2006). Introduction: Nouvelles Recherches sur l'Agriculture Institutionnelle et Domestique en Égypte Ancienne dans le Contexte des Sociétés Antiques. In J. C. Moreno García, ed., *L'Agriculture Institutionnelle en Égypte Ancienne: État de la Question et Perspectives Interdisciplinaires*. Villeneuve d'Ascq: Université Charles-de-Gaulle, Lille III, pp. 11–78.

Moreno García, J. C. (2013). The "Other" Administration: Patronage System and Informal Networks of Power in Ancient Egypt. In J. C. Moreno García, ed., *Ancient Egyptian Administration*. Leiden: Brill, pp. 1029–1065.

Moreno García, J. C. (2017). Trade and Power in Ancient Egypt: Middle Egypt in the Late Third/Early Second Millennium BC. *Journal of Archaeological Research*, **25**(2), 87–132.

Moreno García, J. C. (2019). *The State in Ancient Egypt: Power, Challenges and Dynamics*. London: Bloomsbury.

Moreno García, J. C. (2020). Landscape, Settlement and Populations: Production and Regional Dynamics in Middle Egypt in the *longue durée*. In Th. Schneider, and Ch. Johnston, eds., *The Gift of the Nile? Ancient Egypt and the Environment*. Tucson: University of Arizona Egyptian Expedition, pp. 145–170.

Moreno García, J. C. (2021). Changes and Limits of Royal Taxation in Pharaonic Egypt (2300–2000 BCE). In J. Valk, and I. Soto Marín, eds.,

Ancient Taxation: The Mechanics of Extraction in Comparative Perspective. New York: New York University Press, pp. 290–324.

Moreno García, J. C. (2024). *Dmjw, n(j)wtjw* "townsfolk" in the *Coffin Texts*: Social and political changes in Egypt at the turn of the third millennium BC. In C. Gracia Zamacona, ed., *Variability in the Earlier Egyptian Mortuary Texts (c. 2600–1600 BCE)*. Leiden-Boston: Brill, pp. 190–218.

Mynářová, J., and Alivernini, S., eds. (2020). *Economic Complexity in the Ancient Near East: Management of Resources and Taxation (Third-Second Millenium BC)*. Prague: Charles University.

Oppenheim, A. Oppenheim, A., Arnold, Do., Arnold, Di. and Yamamoto, K., eds. (2015). *Ancient Egypt Transformed: The Middle Kingdom*. New York: The Metropolitan Museum of Art.

Owen, D. I., ed. (2010). *Garšana Studies*. Bethesda: CDL Press.

Parkinson, R. B. (1997). *The Tale of Sinuhe and Other Ancient Egyptian Poems, 1940–1640 BC*. Oxford: Oxford University Press.

Parkinson, R. B. (2002). *Poetry and Culture in Middle Kingdom Egypt: A Dark Side to Perfection*. Sheffield: Equinox.

Petrie, W. M. F. (1888). *A Season in Egypt: 1887*. London: Field & Tuer.

Quirke, S. (1988). State and Labour in the Middle Kingdom: A Reconsideration of the Term *ḫnrt*. *Revue d'Égyptologie*, **39**, 83–106.

Quirke, S., ed. (1991a). *Middle Kingdom Studies*. New Malden: SIA.

Quirke, S. (1991b). Royal Power in the 13th Dynasty. In S. Quirke, ed., *Middle Kingdom Studies*. New Malden: SIA, pp. 123–139.

Quirke, S. (2004a). *Egyptian Literature 1800 BC: Questions and Readings*. London: Golden House.

Quirke, S. (2004b). *Titles and Bureaux of Egypt 1850–1700 BC*. London: Golden House.

Quirke, S. (2016). Who Writes the Literary in Late Middle Kingdom Lahun? In K. Ryholt, and G. Barjamovic, eds., *Problems of Canonicity and Identity Formation in Ancient Egypt and Mesopotamia*. Copenhagen: Museum Tusculanum Press, pp. 127–152.

Quirke, S. (2018). Palace Administration in Middle Kingdom and Second Intermediate Period Egypt. In M. Bietak, and S. Prell, eds., *Ancient Egyptian and Ancient Near Eastern Palaces*, vol. I. Vienna: Austrian Academy of Sciences, pp. 169–221.

Renger, J. (1973). Who Are All Those People? *Orientalia*, **42**, 259–273.

Renger, J. (1994). On Economic Structures in Ancient Mesopotamia: Part One. *Orientalia*, **63**(3), 157–208.

Renger, J. (1995). Institutional, Communal, and Individual Ownership or Possession of Arable Land in Ancient Mesopotamia from the End of the

Fourth to the End of the First Millennium B.C. *Chicago-Kent Law Review*, **71** (1), 269–319.

Richardson, S. (2007). The World of the Babylonian Countrysides. In G. Leick, ed., *The Babylonian World*. London: Routledge, pp. 13–38.

Richardson, S. (2010). *Texts from the Late Old Babylonian Period*. Boston: American Schools of Oriental Research.

Richardson, S. (2012). Early Mesopotamia: The Presumptive State. *Past & Present*, **215**, 3–49.

Richardson, S. (2017). Before Things Worked: A "Low-Power" Model of Early Mesopotamia. In C. Ando, and S. Richardson, eds., *Ancient States and Infrastructural Power: Europe, Asia, and America*. Philadelphia: University of Pennsylvania Press, pp. 17–62.

Richardson, S. (2018). The Mesopotamian Citizen Conceptualized: Affect, Speech and Perception. In J. Brooke, J. C. Strauss, and G. Anderson, eds., *State Formations: Global Histories and Cultures of Statehood*. Cambridge: Cambridge University Press, pp. 261–275.

Richardson, S. (2020). Old Babylonian Taxation as Political Mechanism. In J. Mynářová, and S. Alivernini, eds., *Economic Complexity in the Ancient Near East: Management of Resources and Taxation (Third-Second Millenium BC)*. Prague: Charles University, pp. 217–247.

Richardson, S. (2022). Old Babylonian Letters and Class Formation: Tropes of Sympathy and Social Proximity. *Journal of Ancient History*, **10**(1), 1–34.

Robson, E. (2013). Lone Heroes or Collaborative Communities? On Sumerian Literature and Its Practitioners. In R. Enmarch, and V. Lepper, eds., *Ancient Egyptian Literature: Theory and Practice*. Oxford: Oxford University Press, pp. 45–61.

Roth, M. (1995). *Law Collections from Mesopotamia and Asia Minor*. Atlanta: Society of Biblical Literature.

Sallaberger, W. (1999). *"Wenn Du mein Bruder bist, ... ": Interaktion und Textgestaltung in altbabylonischen Alltagsbriefen*. Leiden: Brill.

Selz, G. (2007). Power, Economy, and Social Organisation in Babylonia. In G. Leick, ed., *The Babylonian World*. London: Routledge, pp. 276–287.

Selz, G. (2010). "The Poor Are the Silent Ones in the Country": On the Loss of Legitimacy; Challenging Power in Early Mesopotamia. In P. Charvát, and P. M. Vlcková, eds., *Who Was King? Who Was Not King? The Rulers and the Ruled in the Ancient Near East*. Prague: Institute of Archaeology of the Academy of Sciences of the Czech Republic, pp. 1–15.

Seri, A. (2005). *Local Power in Old Babylonian Mesopotamia*. Sheffield: Equinox.

Sharlach, T. M. (2004). *Provincial Taxation and the Ur III State*. Leiden: Brill.

Stauder-Porchet, J., Frood, E., and Stauder, A., eds. (2020). *Ancient Egyptian Biographies: Contexts, Forms, Functions*. Atlanta: Lockwood Press.

Steinkeller, P. (2017). An Estimate of the Population of the City of Umma in Ur III Times. In Y. Heffron, A. Stone, and M. Worthington, eds., *At the Dawn of History: Ancient Near Eastern Studies in Honour of J. N. Postgate*. Winona Lake: Eisenbrauns, pp. 535–566.

Stone, E. (1987). *Nippur Neighborhoods*. Chicago: The Oriental Institute of the University of Chicago.

Toonen, H. J. Cortebeeck, K., Hendrickx, S., Bader, B., Peeters, J. and Willems, H. (2022). The Hydro-Geomorphological Setting of the Old Kingdom Town of al-Ashmūnayn in the Egyptian Nile Valley. *Geoarchaeology*, 37(2), 267–283.

Valk, J., and Soto Marín, I., eds. (2021). *Ancient Taxation: The Mechanics of Extraction in Comparative Perspective*. New York: New York University Press.

Van De Mieroop, M. (1992). *Society and Enterprise in Old Babylonian Ur*. Berlin: D. Reimer.

Van De Mieroop, M. (1997). *The Ancient Mesopotamian City*. Oxford: Oxford University Press.

Van den Boorn, G. P. F. (1988). *The Duties of the Vizier: Civil Administration in the Early New Kingdom*. London: Kegan Paul International.

Van Koppen, F. (2011). The Scribe of the Flood Story and His Circle. In K. Radner, and E. Robson, eds., *The Oxford Handbook of Cuneiform Culture*. Oxford: Oxford University Press, pp. 140–166.

Vernus, P. (2010). *Sagesses de l'Égypte Pharaonique*. Arles: Actes Sud.

Von Dassow, E. (2012). The Public and the State in the Ancient Near East. In G. Wilhelm, ed., *Organization, Representation, and Symbols of Power in the Ancient Near East*. Winona Lake: Eisenbrauns, pp. 171–190.

Wegner, J. (2010). External Connections of the Community of Wah-Sut during the Late Middle Kingdom. In Z. A. Hawass, P. Der Manuelian, and R. B. Hussein, eds., *Perspectives on Ancient Egypt: Studies in Honor of Edward Brovarski*. Cairo: Supreme Council of Antiquities, pp. 437–458.

Westbrook, R. (2005). Patronage in the Ancient Near East. *Journal of the Economic and Social History of the Orient*, **48**, 210–233.

Wilhelm, G., ed. (2012). *Organization, Representation, and Symbols of Power in the Ancient Near East*. Winona Lake: Eisenbrauns.

Willems, H. (2014). *Historical and Archaeological Aspects of Egyptian Funerary Culture: Religious Ideas and Ritual Practice in Middle Kingdom Elite Cemeteries*. Leiden: Brill.

Yoffee, N. (1977). *The Economic Role of the Crown in the Old Babylonian Period*. Malibu: Undena.

Yoffee, N. (1998). The Economics of Ritual at Late Old Babylonian Kish. *Journal of the Economic and Social History of the Orient*, **41**, 312–343.

To José Enrique Peña García for his lifelong fraternal, supporting and loyal friendship, always present in times of doubt and hardship.

Cambridge Elements

Ancient Egypt in Context

Gianluca Miniaci
University of Pisa

Gianluca Miniaci is Associate Professor in Egyptology at the University of Pisa, Honorary Researcher at the Institute of Archaeology, UCL – London, and Chercheur associé at the École Pratique des Hautes Études, Paris. He is currently co-director of the archaeological mission at Zawyet Sultan (Menya, Egypt). His main research interest focuses on the social history and the dynamics of material culture in Middle Bronze Age Egypt and its interconnections between the Levant, Aegean, and Nubia.

Juan Carlos Moreno García
CNRS, Paris

Juan Carlos Moreno García (PhD in Egyptology, 1995) is a CNRS senior researcher at the Sorbonne University, as well as lecturer on social and economic history of ancient Egypt at the École des Hautes Études en Sciences Sociales (EHESS) in Paris. He has published extensively on the administration, socio-economic history, and landscape organization of ancient Egypt, usually in a comparative perspective with other civilizations of the ancient world, and has organized several conferences on these topics.

Anna Stevens
University of Cambridge and Monash University

Anna Stevens is a research archaeologist with a particular interest in how material culture and urban space can shed light on the lives of the non-elite in ancient Egypt. She is Senior Research Associate at the McDonald Institute for Archaeological Research and Assistant Director of the Amarna Project (both University of Cambridge).

About the Series

The aim of this Elements series is to offer authoritative but accessible overviews of foundational and emerging topics in the study of ancient Egypt, along with comparative analyses, translated into a language comprehensible to non-specialists. Its authors will take a step back and connect ancient Egypt to the world around, bringing ancient Egypt to the attention of the broader humanities community and leading Egyptology in new directions.

Cambridge Elements

Ancient Egypt in Context

Elements in the Series

Ceramic Perspectives on Ancient Egyptian Society
Leslie Anne Warden

The Nile: Mobility and Management
Judith Bunbury and Reim Rowe

The Archaeology of Egyptian Non-Royal Burial Customs in New Kingdom Egypt and Its Empire
Wolfram Grajetzki

Power and Regions in Ancient States
Gary M. Feinman and Juan Carlos Moreno García

Ancient Egypt in Its African Context: Economic Networks, Social and Cultural Interactions
Andrea Manzo

Egyptian Archaeology and the Twenty-First-Century Museum
Alice Stevenson

Technology and Culture in Pharaonic Egypt: Actor Network Theory and the Archaeology of Things and People
Martin Fitzenreiter

Famine and Feast in Ancient Egypt
Ellen Morris

Hieroglyphs, Pseudo-Scripts and Alphabets: Their Use and Reception in Ancient Egypt and Neighbouring Regions
Ben Haring

Scribal Culture in Ancient Egypt
Niv Allon and Hana Navratilova

Making Memories in Ancient Egypt
Leire Olabarria

Monarchies and the Organization of Power: Ancient Egypt and Babylonia Compared (2100–1750 BC)
Juan Carlos Moreno García and Seth Richardson

A full series listing is available at: www.cambridge.org/AECE

For EU product safety concerns, contact us at Calle de José Abascal, 56–1°, 28003 Madrid, Spain or eugpsr@cambridge.org.

www.ingramcontent.com/pod-product-compliance
Lightning Source LLC
LaVergne TN
LVHW020349260326
834688LV00045B/1628